AMÉ...

AND THE TALB...

FROM THE JOURNALS OF AMÉLINA PETIT DE BILLIER

Translated and selected by Sheila Metcalf and Trudy Wallace

MADEIRA ROAD MEDIA

Published in Great Britain in 2012 by Madeira Road Media (MADEIRA.ROAD@virginmedia.com).

ISBN 978-0-9573005-0-7

COVER IMAGE
Lacock Abbey from a print of 1847
Amélina with Caroline (seated) and Horatia, from a photograph taken by William Henry Fox Talbot in the 1840s
TITLE PAGE IMAGE
A recently discovered photograph of Amélina Petit de Billier in advanced years. 'I remember her in her armchair, with a soft white wrap round her shoulders [...], and I noticed her bright dark eyes and wavy white hair.' Matilda Talbot from *My Life at Lacock Abbey*
FACING PAGE
Amélina from a photograph by William Henry Fox Talbot taken in the 1840s
Some of the contents of Amélina's portable writing desk

Typeset in Garamond
Printed and bound by CPI Group (UK) Ltd, Croydon CRO 4YY

Designed by Jude Harris

The extracts from the journals of Amélina Petit de Billier which we have included in this volume were selected to illustrate her experiences as a much-loved companion to the family of William Henry Fox Talbot at Lacock Abbey.

Amélina's spelling occasionally shows some inconsistencies which we have not attempted to standardise (for example, she refers both to Laycock and to Lacock). Some short passages in her journals were written in English and these are indicated in the text by the lighter type also used for this sentence. Amélina also used some Italian expressions and these we have retained while also providing an English translation [in square brackets]. In later life Amélina revised parts of her journals, occasionally adding new material: an example of this is found in square brackets on page 35 of this volume. The text includes three quotations taken from *The Correspondence of William Henry Fox Talbot*, available online as part of the Talbot Correspondence Project directed by Larry J. Schaaf (foxtalbot.dmu.ac.uk).

We should like to express our gratitude to the following for their invaluable assistance at various stages of our work: the late Janet Burnett-Brown for her help and encouragement from the outset and not least for her pioneering work on an English translation of the journals; our excellent designer Jude Harris; the Collections team at the Bath Royal Literary and Scientific Institution, which hosted the project; the National Trust at Lacock, especially Graham Heard; Roger Watson, Curator of the Fox Talbot Museum, Lacock; John Falconer, Lead Curator Visual Arts and Curator of Photographs at the British Library; Michael Gray, the independent curator and Talbot expert; Rachel Hunt, House and Collections Manager at Cotehele House; Dr Kate Fielden, Curator at Bowood House; and Professor Ian Wallace.

Sheila Metcalf and Trudy Wallace

CONTENTS

(1) William Davenport Talbot = Lady Elisabeth = (2) Admiral Charles
(1763–1800) Fox-Strangways Feilding
Lady Elisabeth's first husband (m. 1796). *(1773–1846)* *(1780–1837)*
Captain in the 88th Foot Regiment, who *Eldest daughter of 2nd* *Her second marriage in 1804 was to*
inherited Lacock Abbey on death of his *Earl of Ilchester.* *Capt. Charles Feilding, later Rear*
uncle John Talbot in 1778. *Also referred to as* *Admiral (1780–1837). Stepfather*
Father of William Henry Fox Talbot. *Lady Feilding, Lady E.* *of William Henry Fox Talbot and*
father of Caroline and Horatia
Feilding.

William Henry Fox Talbot **Caroline** **Horatia**
(1800–77) *(1808–81)* *(1810–51)*
Pioneer Photographer *First daughter of Lady Elisabeth* *Second daughter of Lady Elisabeth*
who inherited Lacock Abbey in 1821. *Theresa Fox-Strangways and* *Theresa Fox-Strangways and Charles*
Married Constance Mundy (1811–1880) *Charles Feilding. Married in* *Feilding. Married Capt. Thomas*
of Markeaton in 1832. W.H.Fox Talbot *1831 to Ernest Augustus Valletort* *Gaisford (1816–1898). Horatia died*
and Constance Mundy had four children: *(1797–1861), 3rd Earl of Mount* *after giving birth to a boy, Horace*
Ela Theresa Talbot (1835–1893) *Edgcumbe. They had two children:* *Charles Gaisford (1851–1879).*
Rosamond Constance Talbot (1837–1906) *William Henry (1832–1917)*
Matilda Caroline Talbot (1839–1927) *4th Earl of Edgcumbe*
Charles Henry Talbot (1842–1916) *Lady Ernestine Emma Horatia*
(1843–1925)

The Talbots and the Feildings – Amélina's English families. Amélina *(seated on the right)* is shown
photographed with Horatia Feilding and an unidentified person, possibly Amélina's maid

Amélina
and the Talbot Family

With what emotion did I find myself again within the hospitable walls of this old abbey, to which so many interesting memories are attached! I have had such happy times here.
Amélina Petit de Billier, 10 September 1831

A mong the treasures of Lacock Abbey in Wiltshire are fifteen worn notebooks, the journals of Amélina Petit de Billier. Written in French, with a few entries in English or Italian, and covering the period from 1820 to 1835, they afford invaluable insights into Amélina's life with the Talbot family at Lacock Abbey between 1827 and 1835, including her often frank and refreshing view of places and events, and her unusual and privileged glimpses of the great or famous.

Amélina was born in Paris on 30 May 1798 and died at Lacock on 8 September 1876. Beyond the fact that she had two brothers and that her mother remarried in 1826, very little is known about her early years, and the precise circumstances in which she left her family in Paris in 1820 to join the Feilding family in England also remain unknown. Indeed, the only strong clue we have about her early life is her reference to 'Mme Vigogne, to whom I owe the cultivation of my mind, my intelligence and my very feeble talents'. Can this be the Mme Vigogne who ran the school at the Quai de Billy in Paris attended by daughters of members of the Emperor Napoleon's court?

The Feilding family consisted of Charles Feilding, a retired naval captain (and eventually a Rear-Admiral), his wife Lady Elisabeth, his stepson William Henry Fox Talbot, and his two daughters, Caroline and Horatia. Charles Feilding was very well-connected, while his wife Lady Elisabeth ('Milady') was the daughter of the second Earl of Ilchester. Many of her family lived in grand country houses: her sister Lady Lansdowne at Bowood, another sister Mary (married to another Talbot) at Penrice in Wales, her stepmother at Abbotsbury, and her half-brother (the third Earl) at Melbury. William Henry, the son of Lady Elisabeth's first marriage, became heir to Lacock Abbey as an infant of six months when his father died in 1800. As is well known, he became famous in due course as the inventor of the calotype and the negative-positive method of photography, and he is now celebrated in the National Trust Museum attached to the Abbey.

It has been assumed that Amélina was originally engaged as governess to the two girls, but no lessons whether in music or in any of the other usual accomplishments are ever mentioned, and she seems from the outset to have lived as one of the family. Whatever her exact status (in the 1851 census she was categorised as 'Visitor'), it is clear that Amélina Petit de Billier did have to sing for her supper, but she did it successfully with voice, harp or piano, in the company of such

Lacock Abbey, showing the west entrance *(on the left)* and Sharington Tower *(on the right)*

well-known figures as Thomas Moore, with professionals, and with aristocratic amateurs, in the best country houses and the highest social circles of London, Paris, Nice, Florence, Venice and Rome. Nor did she neglect the opportunities which such journeyings brought her. Evidently blessed with a lively intellect and a thorough education in the arts, she revelled in opera, theatre, museums, libraries, and intelligent conversation, as well as the usual tourist attractions (and some of the more unusual ones), the parties, the riding and hunting, the dancing and the charades.

On her arrival in England in 1820 Amélina was first introduced for a few weeks to the sights of London, where the trial of Queen Caroline was giving rise to noisy demonstrations in her favour. These even followed them when they left for a round of country house visits:

> On the road the country people surrounded our carriage to make us shout 'Long live the Queen'. We slept at Andover and we were assailed by an immense crowd of people who wanted the inn to be lit up; the landlord [was] quite a peaceable man, with the reputation of being opposed to the reformers, so all of a sudden stones began raining on the windows which they broke, coming into the sitting room where we were taking tea; we were overcome by fear.

In a letter now in the Talbot correspondence, Lady Elisabeth writes to her son:

> Mlle Amélina was in great astonishment tho' she had often heard of the liberty of England, but would not believe it. She preserved a stone to shew in France, where they always imagine such things cannot be without a revolution.

With a diversion for Amélina to see Stonehenge, they went on to visit the country houses of Lady Elisabeth's sisters, aunt, and stepmother. These included Melbury and Stinsford as well as Abbotsbury, where, to Amélina's astonishment, one of Lady Elisabeth's sisters, Lady Henrietta Frampton, showed her a lock of Napoleon's hair which Amélina describes as 'fine and soft as silk'. Amélina tells us that Lady Henrietta had received this gift from the wife of the General who was the commander at St. Helena. After visiting Stourhead, 'the charming mansion

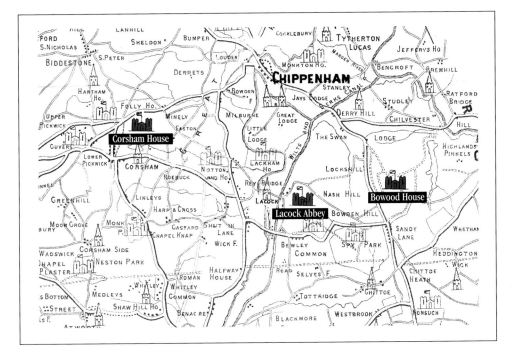

The locations of Lacock Abbey, Bowood House, Corsham House and many of the places nearby mentioned in Amélina's journals.

of Sir Richard Hoare', she marvelled at the Marquis of Bath's 'magnificent house (at Longleat), furnished with a richness which I have never before found in this country'.

They arrived at Bowood for Christmas. Here she met her first celebrity, Maria Edgeworth 'with whom I had much conversation'. Miss Edgeworth does not record this in her *Letters from England* when describing her visit to one of her sisters, but only comments on the Feildings: Lady Elisabeth 'more affected than at Paris, and full of dress and Venetian bracelets etc.' and Mr Feilding 'very gentleman-like and agreeable'. Back in London for several weeks, the entertainments included concerts, sightseeing, art collections, Covent Garden, and the British Museum, newly-founded in temporary premises and unimpressive: 'not well looked after, without order and in a mean smoke-blackened building, [with] very few objects of each kind'.

In February 1821 Henry Talbot reached his majority and inherited the Lacock estate, but the Abbey was let on a lease, and the Feildings were obliged to spend the next six years in London in Mr Feilding's house at 31 Sackville Street, or travelling, until they were at last able to take possession of the estate in August 1827.

For four years, from 1821–5, the Feilding family travelled and lived in Europe. The main party of Mr Feilding, Lady Elisabeth, Caroline, Horatia, and Amélina was augmented from time to time by Henry Talbot, Mr Fazakerly, a friend of Mr Feilding's; and the Rev. George Montgomerie, a friend of the family with a living in Norfolk. They went first from Paris to Berne, for four months, then to Nice for the winter;

Florence for six months, Rome for another six, the Italian Lakes, the following winter in Genoa, then via Venice, Vienna and Munich to Paris for the winter of 1824–5. In this way periods of travelling were interspersed with lengthy periods in rented houses, and wherever they went they found fellow-travellers or residents from England.

In November 1823 they arrived in Genoa and inspected houses for rent.

We went up to the charming hill of Albaro, to see the house occupied by Lord Byron and Mme Guiccioli, née Gamba, during the long stay he made in this town: he has left there his furniture and his library, which is numerous, particularly for a man who leads a wandering life, and he had even kept the house at his disposal, but he has written lately to the owner giving him permission to rent it, if the occasion arose, and it was with the intention of living there that Mr F. took us there, at least if it could be arranged. [...] It is quite big, but in very bad order, and is clearly the dwelling of a poet. I went over it with great interest: the garden seat shaded by olive trees, where he passed hours in meditation; the big chair in which he preferred to sit; the table where he composed some of his vigorous poems; his books; his portrait; that of his daughter; all this attracted our attention. He has left some fine furniture there, but in the greatest disorder. His spirit was too far above the little things of domestic life; to take care of those he left this duty to some people with whom, it appears, he came to regret surrounding himself. Lord B. is impulsive, a natural consequence of a passionate imagination. He allowed himself to be surrounded, and almost dominated by so-called friends, who at heart were nothing but parasites, who were, they say, people completely without principles, adventurers attaching themselves where they could. In the end he was disabused, though rather late. They think that he has undertaken his journey to Greece with the intention of casting them off, and he has succeeded, but I consider that this misconstrues the fine motive which caused his action: devoted to the Greeks, and the great days of their liberty, he wished to take part in giving back to the Greeks of today that precious liberty, trampled underfoot for centuries in that unhappy country. [...] The owner Mr Barry told us that he had been accustomed to spend an hour each day, working on one of his poems, which were worth their weight in gold; for he has become rather more calculating, and makes a profit from his works. It is true that this is so that he can use it nobly now. They say that he is impatiently waiting for his daughter Ada to reach her seventh year, to take her from her mother, from whom he separated after two years of marriage, the laws of England only permitting it then. Lady Byron anticipates this with despair. Lady Byron is a rich heiress, who wished to marry him to satisfy her vanity, but she is well paid for her folly! Poets are rarely good husbands!

Their travels in their own carriage, with servants (including a French cook) and a courier, were nevertheless plagued by the drawbacks and disasters common to all such travels: innkeepers, postmasters, and frontier guards (mainly Austrian) harrassed them, the inns were often dirty, the food poor (so that they frequently carried their own provisions with them) and the weather often treacherous, but through it all they seem to have been on cordial terms with each other, with

Left to right: The Irish writer Maria Edgeworth (1768-1849) whom Amélina met at Bowood House in 1820; the composer Giacchino Rossini (1792-1868) whose work she greatly admired; and the celebrated opera singer Giuditta Pasta (1797-1865) whom she heard many times in Milan, London, and Paris.

occasional disagreements quickly resolved. They often split up into two or three groups for different excursions, sometimes for several days, in any number of different permutations, and evidently with great pleasure in each other's company and in their new experiences (even a descent into the salt mines of Salzburg).

When they settled in a city, they undertook a gruelling social and cultural programme. In Nice, Amélina danced with the Sardinian officers 'till stiff all over'; in Rome, 'on Sundays the church of St Peter contains all the London fashionables, who meet there to talk of yesterday's ball and tomorrow's play, to look at the pretty women, laugh, promenade, stare and gossip loudly, arm in arm', and their dinner guests included the Duke of Devonshire, the French Ambassador (the Duc de Laval-Montmorency) and many friends from England.

With opera, concerts, theatres and dinners by night, their days were filled with sightseeing. Amélina's room-by-room record of the contents of art galleries and studios (including, in Rome, those of Thorwaldsen and Canova) testifies not only to her enthusiasm but to her knowledge and judgement. However it is for music above all that she felt the deepest response, especially for opera, and above all for Rossini. In Paris, in February 1825, she was thrilled to see and hear him at a private concert.

> I went to Mrs Wilkinson's fine concert: a great many people of the *beau monde* of every country were there. I was in a state of delight throughout all the music: Rossini! accompanied the singers on the piano! He is excessively fat, and his countenance not very expressive, although his features are handsome, but he looks good-natured, and his manners are sociable. He played the piano marvellously, and how well he showed off his own music! Mme Pasta was charming yesterday, and sang like an angel, especially the famous aria by Gluck 'J'ai perdu mon Euridice', in Italian. She was well dressed, and looked very distinguished. Rossini on the piano, and Lafond on the violin played a delightful duet on the *Rondo of Emma* by Auber.

The guests included Prince Leopold of Saxe-Coburg (not yet King of the Belgians but Princess Charlotte's widower), M. Rothschild, and the Duchesse de Castries. A month later she heard 'young Liszt, a prodigy about fourteen or fifteen years old, [who] improvised on the piano in an extraordinary manner. He has perfect technique'.

While seeming less interested in the performing arts than Amélina and the rest of the family, Henry Talbot did pursue the longstanding interest in the sciences which he had already evinced as a schoolboy. In Germany he met the famous explorers Chamisso and Alexander von Humboldt, and Amélina writes of luncheons at which important scientists were present, for example in Munich where the famous botanist C.F.P. von Martius and the noted physicist Fraunhofer were present along with John Herschel. On 19 September 1824 she notes:

> Mr. Fraunhofer, astronomer of Munich, has also dined with us, he too is very 'savant' with lots of simplicity and bonhomie: he has discovered a lot and made the most perfect instruments which one now knows in Europe. [...] Mr. Talbot says he considers Mr. Fraunhofer one of the greatest living astronomers.

While in Paris in February 1825, on the way back to England, the family met the famous French physicist and astronomer Arago while walking in the Tuileries, and we know from Talbot's own journal that later, in March of the same year, Talbot spent several days with Arago in the Paris Observatory.

Napoleon was a tragic hero to Amélina. His death in 1821 prompted an outburst of grief, and she eulogises him on many occasions when confronted by his likeness all over Europe. It was therefore a high point in her life when in Venice in 1824 she was introduced to his sister.

> Spent the evening at Lady Westmorland's to meet the ex-Queen of Naples, Caroline Murat, Napoleon's sister. [...] I was much moved on seeing her: she is very much changed, but she has kept her charming figure, dazzling skin, the most beautiful shoulders I have ever seen, a graceful neck, the prettiest little hand, a pretty foot, fine teeth, the most animated countenance, the sweetest voice. [...] All the company was presented. She is treated with great deference and respect here. Mr F. spoke to her about me, and of how I had wished to see her. At once she crossed the group, came and sat down by me, and began with such ease, such an attractive and unaffected manner, that I felt I was meeting an old acquaintance. We talked a great deal! [...] Poor woman, what sorrows she has had! The conversation was sometimes difficult, there are so many matters I dared not touch on, but I talked with her about Naples, about Portici, about the young Napoleon, and her children: her elder son is, she told me, in America. Her other son Prince Achille was there: he is 21, with a very handsome face, but unfortunately he is much too fat, and has rather a vulgar appearance. However, when he talks, the bad impression goes away, for he expresses himself very well, and like a distinguished man. [...]

> Queen Caroline asked me to sing, and I wanted to oblige her, but our hostess had not asked me to, when young Prince Achille came to beg me, on behalf of all the company, to make myself heard. I agreed, and he led me by the hand to the piano, where M. Perruchini, a very distinguished amateur musician accompanied me. I sang first the prayer from *Otello*, and then the lovely song Elena in which I recovered from my foolish nervousness, and acquitted myself better than I could have believed. [...] Prince Achille came to stand by me, and paid me many compliments, and asked his mother to thank me. Then we waltzed and danced. Prince Achille waltzes very well: he asked Caroline, and then her sister. I played the harp a little.

Marc Brunel's Thames Tunnel. '30 August 1826: Saw the tunnel under the Thames. It is a bold enterprise to have a passage under such a river, however they have made great progress.'

When the Feildings returned to England in 1825, Amélina was a woman in her mid-twenties, tied closely to the family through four years of shared experiences, confident in society, and forthright in her opinions concerning art, politics and people, her command of English and Italian now sure enough to allow her to fall into either language when it seemed appropriate. Equally Caroline and Horatia were now no longer children, but young ladies, ready to be presented at court.

In London she found 'smoke, fog etc, as usual' but also 'the city much improved by a superb street which crosses a great part of it, called Regent Street'. Here they mixed with the same society and saw the same operas, sung by the same singers, as they had been enjoying on the Continent.

> We went to the opera in Mrs Hope's box, expecting to see *Semiramide*, but a notice inside announced *Otello*. The public who had not seen the notice (put up very late according to what is said) rose suddenly in indignation when the curtain, rising, displayed St. Mark's Square, the Doge, and the Venetian Senate, then cries of off! off! broke out on all sides [...] and after many coming and goings a young man appeared who explained that because of a dispute with Mme Vestris they were not able to give *Semiramide* that evening. The debate lasted an hour and a quarter, some making speeches and interrogating and shouting at the poor substitute for Mr Ebers, whom they had not been able to find; others calling out to proceed, others persisting in rejecting *Otello* and wanting what they called an apology on the part of the director. Finally after a last attempt by the young man, sent no doubt by Mr Ebers, whom they claimed not to be able to find, the opera was allowed to begin, and the rest of the piece passed quietly. Mme Pasta sang divinely, but did not act as well, it seemed to me, as in Paris.

For two years they lived mainly in London, while Amélina saw and commented on everything: Hampton Court, the new Horticultural Gardens, the elder Brunel's Thames Tunnel then under construction, Charles Kemble as Mark Antony, Edmund Kean as Othello, Sir Thomas Lawrence's studio, every possible art exhibition. From time to time they also rented houses in Bristol, Worthing and Brighton for extended stays. While in Bristol Mr Feilding took Amélina on her first visit to Bath on 15 September 1825:

> Mr. F. was kind enough to take me on a little journey to Bath, which is only 12

miles from here and which I wanted to see. The countryside one passes through between Bristol and Bath is pleasant, well cultivated, quite hilly and though it has no outstanding beauty, nature extends its richness and grace there. Bath, a very ancient Roman town, where the Romans already had recognised the virtue of its mineral waters, is quite a big town: it is well built, entirely in cut stone, and situated on a hill which is less steep than Clifton, but quite high. There are very nice shops, fine streets, Bond Street as in London. Invalids come here in the winter and enjoy the mildness of its climate and in summer take the baths and drink the thermal mineral waters, which have great properties. We explored the city all day in full sun and I was very tired from having gone up to Lansdown Crescent which is at the top of the hill. The second (Royal) Crescent is magnificent, very extensive and dominates the town and the valley; it can be seen from a long way away (it is a great regular building in the form of a crescent composed of many beautiful houses rented to visitors). There are several of these crescents; but this is the most beautiful: the Circus has the honours of the three orders of architecture; and also an attractive appearance; we walked in North Parade and South Parade, and saw the private and public baths; the water is naturally very hot: in the public bath everyone bathes together in a big pool, men and women in bedgowns of wool. Previously one dined there; the ladies came, their hair dressed with flowers, feathers, pearls and now everyone rather conceals herself. There is a beautiful ballroom which holds 500 people; a concert hall, a meeting hall, one for gaming; there is much amusement here in the winter but gaming (roulette), which was the greatest attraction of these waters, completely disappeared seven or eight years ago, public gambling being forbidden.

The library there has been newly created: it contains excellent works in English and French, plaster copies of famous statues, there are several rooms where one can meet; one room where courses and lectures are held. The Marquis of Lansdowne is President of the Society which has made this useful and pleasant establishment. Indeed it seemed to me that one could spend time very well in Bath. There is a Billiard Room. The Pump Room is also a place for meeting. There is music every day; it would have to be very powerful if it could make attractive the water which one drinks, I tasted some; it is very bad, warm, with a bitter metallic taste. We dined in Sidney Gardens; gardens like those at Vauxhall where parties are given: they commended to us its excellent French chef and his à la carte dinners, but we found nothing but a bad female English cook and had a plain dinner: I was so tired that I did not mind; afterwards we walked and went on the swings, we went back to Bristol in a diligence to see the famous grey horse of the postmaster.

In August 1827 the Talbots were at last able to take possession of the Lacock estate, and during their first winter there, they established a new life of local visits, village charity, and country pursuits which Amélina unexpectedly enjoyed.

Lady Elisabeth's sister Louisa had married the Marquess of Lansdowne and was consequently the mistress of Bowood House, a few miles from Lacock. The two families exchanged visits constantly and enjoyed the frequent company of Thomas Moore, the Irish poet, who lived nearby and was much prized at Bowood. They became closely acquainted with English politics owing to Lord Lansdowne's importance as a member of successive governments and later to Henry Talbot's brief

term as MP for Chippenham from 1832. Amélina had always recorded political events in her journal, but while French and Russian politics were probably gleaned from the newspapers, English politics, and particularly the events leading up to the Catholic Emancipation and Reform Bills, are often reported from personal knowledge, both in Wiltshire and in London.

After visiting her family in Paris, in July 1828 Amélina went to live with the Hopwood family at Hopwood Hall, a few miles from Manchester. Just as her recruitment into the Feilding family is not explained in the journals (nor in any letters in the Talbot correspondence), so there is no explanation of why or how the new arrangement arose. She maintained a loving correspondence with all the Feildings, and evidently compared the Hopwood family unfavourably with them. Mr Hopwood lacked Mr Feilding's kind concern for her welfare, Mrs Hopwood, of uncertain temper and limited culture, lacked Lady Elisabeth's aristocratic style, and her daughter Mary, who was constantly ailing, appears to have lacked the charm and talents of the Feilding girls. They did, however, belong to grand social circles, and the exchange of visits with Lord and Lady Wilton of Heaton Hall, Lord Molyneux, the heir of Croxteth, whom Mary eventually married, and the Stanleys of Knowsley, together with race meetings, and holidays in the Lake District and Anglesey, provided Amélina with lively material for her diary. However, in 1831, her health broke down, and in September of that year she fled to Lacock to recuperate. 'I crept about in the garden, for that is all I am able to do. [...] I have only a faint hope that I shall ever recover.' She improved only slowly but was soon totally absorbed in the engagement and marriage of Caroline Feilding to Lord Valletort, heir to the Earl of Mount Edgcumbe, godson and aide-de-camp to William IV, which took place in December in the chapel at Bowood.

By March 1832, Amélina was well enough to travel to Paris, to spend several months with her family. On her return she enjoyed a short time in Lacock and London with the Feildings, remaining until after Caroline gave birth to her first son in November ('one of the sweetest moments of my life'). She returned to Hopwood but in January 1833 was delighted to receive an invitation from Henry Talbot, (who had recently been elected MP for Chippenham, and married) to join him and his bride on a continental tour.

On this tour Amélina revisited many of the places she already knew from her travels with the elder Feildings in 1821–5. Henry Talbot was not such an easy travelling companion, being more interested in botanising than the arts, and Amélina and Constance, his wife, occasionally rebelled, but she had the delight of joining Caroline, with Lord Valletort and the baby (affectionately known as Bimbo, later fourth Earl of Mount Edgcumbe) in Varese, Milan, Genoa and Nice. Caroline had always been a talented sketcher of people and places and so was Talbot's wife, Constance, though Talbot was not. He himself has recorded that this tour inspired the research which resulted within a few years in his photographic method. According to his book *The Pencil of Nature* (1844-6) it was on Lake Como in 1833 that – to use his words: 'The idea occurred to me [...] how charming it would be if it were possible to cause these natural images to imprint themselves durably, and remain fixed upon the paper.'

Amélina's return to Hopwood in May 1834 was enlivened by Mary Hopwood's marriage to Lord Molyneux, Lord Sefton's heir, in July. When she returned to Paris the following year, and finished the fifteenth volume of her journals, it seems that Amélina feared her connection with Lacock and the Feilding family might be at an end. In fact she was to be intimately involved with Henry Talbot's family for most of the rest of her life, as his business agent in Paris when he began to market his photographic method, and then at Lacock as companion to his wife and children. She re-read her journals in 1870, adding some comments and making many deletions.

On 8th September 1876 she died an honoured member of the Talbot household and was buried in Lacock churchyard in the Talbot family grave. The family was deeply affected, as a letter which Talbot wrote on the day of her death to the Lacock stewart, Mr. West Awdry, makes clear: 'You will be sorry to hear that our hopes for the recovery of our dear friend Madame Petit have proved delusive. She died at 4 o'clock this afternoon after an illness of more than two months. The ladies of my family are in great grief, their friendship having been of many years' duration.'

Many years later, Matilda Talbot, the grand-daughter of William Henry Fox Talbot who inherited Lacock Abbey in 1916 and later passed it to the National Trust, wrote a fitting tribute to Amélina in her memoir *My Life at Lacock Abbey*:

Another person I remember at Lacock was the old French governess, Mme Petit. Lalla was the name we children knew her by, but her friends called her 'Mamie,' 'Amandier,' and made other affectionate variants of her real name Amélina. I only saw her that once, but all the same she was an influence in my life. I remember her in her armchair, with a soft white wrap round her shoulders, sitting in what is still called the Upper East Bedroom at Lacock Abbey, and I noticed her bright dark eyes and wavy white hair. She first came to Lacock through some friend of our great-grandmother, Lady Elisabeth, to teach my grandfather's half-sisters, Caroline and Horatia Feilding, and they owed a great deal to her. She had a fine voice and played both the piano and the harp; her harp is still at Lacock. She spoke Italian as well as she did her native French, and she also spoke German, which was not usual at that date. Her full name was Mlle Amélina Petit-de-Billier, but when the family fortunes had sunk low and she was obliged to take a post as governess in England she thought it best just to call herself Madame Petit. When Caroline and Horatia were both grown-up and married, she returned to Paris for a time, but the family at Lacock greatly missed her, and when my grandfather's childen were old enough to need a governess, he persuaded her to come back to teach them, and she remained at Lacock for the rest of her life.

It must have been a rather unusual household to which she returned; my great-grandmother, Lady Elisabeth, and her second husband, Admiral Feilding, my grandfather and his young wife, who was the actual mistress of the house, and their four young children. Mme Petit was a woman of many interests, deep religious convictions and great breadth of view, so that she helped her pupils in many ways besides music, languages and general education. She did not draw, so an artist came over from Bath to teach drawing and painting. Although my mother married when she was twenty and by that time schoolroom days were already over, there was no question of Lalla ever leaving them. They were all much too fond of her. There seems to have been no kind of jealous feeling at all on my grandmother's part that the children should be so devoted to their governess; they were all happy together. To us nowadays it seems strange that when Madame Petit first came to Lacock as a governess, she brought her maid with her, one Henriette Sanit, quite a young girl. Henriette had married unhappily, her husband drank and ill-treated her, so she fled back to her parents and then took service with Lalla. Henriette also soon became a valuable member of the household. She was a clever dressmaker and both witty and amusing. I remember her well, for she used to come and stay with us both in London and in Scotland. It must have been about six months after our return to Scotland from my first visit to Lacock, that we had the news of Lalla's death. She had then reached the age of seventy-eight. My mother was deeply grieved and Aunt Rosamond even more so, for she had been in constant attendance on her beloved old governess, more especially when Lalla became ill and weak during the last month of her life.

NORTH PARADE AND LITERARY INSTITUTION, BATH.

North Parade and the Literary Institution, Bath – 'the library there has been newly created: it contains excellent works in English and French, [and] plaster copies of famous statues' as Amélina noted after her first visit to Bath on 15 September 1825

Sydney Gardens, Bath – 'gardens like those at Vauxhall where parties are given' (15 September 1825)

Above left
Caroline Mount
Edgcumbe, née
Feilding

Below left
Dining room, Lacock
Abbey. '10 January
1832: Breakfast
for twelve people
crowded round the
table.'

Above right
Horatia Feilding
(from a photograph
of 1 May 1843). '14
December 1831:
Played duets for
harp and piano with
Horatia and several
tunes from operas
from memory.'

Above
Lacock Abbey's Érard
harp. Amélina praises
'the excellent harp by
Érard, which Mr F.
bought before leaving
London. It is a
perfect instrument.'
(14 August 1827)

Left
William Henry
Fox Talbot
(daguerreotype,
1840)

Below
Drawing of
Lake Como
by Constance
Talbot, wife of
William Henry
Fox Talbot,
made during
their visit to
Italy in autumn
1833

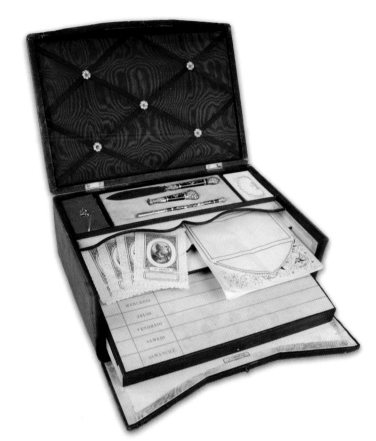

Above right
Amélina's
portable writing-
desk, recently
discovered at
Lacock Abbey

Below right
In 1876 Amélina's
name was
the first to be
inscribed on the
Talbot family
gravestones in
Lacock

From the JOURNALS of

Amélina

William Henry Fox Talbot, the renowned pioneer of photography, was Lady Elisabeth Feilding's son by her first marriage. He inherited the Lacock Estate as a baby on his father's death in 1800. When he reached his majority in 1821, the estate, at first encumbered by debt, was let to tenants on a lease which did not expire until 1827.

The family had visited Lacock when staying with Lady Elisabeth's brother-in-law and sister, Lord and Lady Lansdowne, at Bowood for Christmas 1820. Amélina recorded the visit in her journal, but, surprisingly, declined to go to Lacock with them. She recorded a tradition which she heard while staying with the Marquess of Bath at Longleat on the way to Bowood.

14 December 1820. Someone told us it was said that one tower of Laycock Abbey was haunted by ghosts, and that this tower, which had not been opened for a long time, would only be opened on the day of the majority of the owner, Mr Henry Talbot, the son of Lady Elisabeth. Laycock Abbey is 3 or 4 miles from Bowood.

Saturday 23 December 1820. Mr Feilding, Lady Elis[abeth]. and the young ladies have gone today to visit Laycock Abbey. I declined to make this little expedition, which held little interest for me.

In August 1827 the family came to live at Lacock for the first time.

Saturday 4 August 1827. Left Reading; dined at Marlborough in a pleasant inn where there is a garden and a very large Barrow, ancient tomb of the Danes who fought so much for possession of this country. Arrived at Laycock Abbey at 5 pm. Immediately toured the house, the cloisters, the courtyards, the garden etc. A very interesting ancient abbey founded by Ela Countess of Salisbury in 1229. She had married William Longespee, son of King Henry II and of the Fair Rosamund. One can still see in the cloister the stone which covers the tomb of this foundress, who died there one year after the establishment of the convent of Augustinian nuns. Several members of that family entered the convent. At the Reformation King Henry VIII, having abolished the monasteries, made a present of this one (or at least sold it for very little), with the lands that went with it, to Sir William Sherrington, whose daughter and heiress, Olive, married a Talbot, to whom passed all the riches of this house, and who have kept them to this day. This family of Talbots is also very ancient, from Normandy. One of them is mentioned in the reign of William the Conqueror. Nothing could be more picturesque than the cloister; its elegant

Sharington
Tower at
Lacock Abbey,
built about 1550
by William
Sharington

Gothic arches are covered with ivy: the windows of our bedrooms are like nests in the foliage; we have a very beautiful view of Bowden Hill with Mrs Dickinson's park. Two galleries full of old family portraits, an old library. There are many repairs to be made; the house has fallen into disrepair during Mr Talbot's long minority, but it has plenty to make it a pleasant place to stay.

∽ *Sunday 5 August.* We all went to church, whose exterior is very old. The clergyman is Mr Paley, son of the famous Archdeacon Paley of Carlisle. He looks very respectable, he has a beautiful voice and says the prayers very well. He preached for three quarters of an hour! trying to prevent the villagers from going to the Methodist meetings in their chapel at Laycock. A walk in the three kitchen gardens, where there are very fine fruits, although the garden has been very neglected by an old gardener and even more by Mr Grossett. A walk to Innwood with Mr Felps.

∽ *Monday 6 August.* Lord Kerry came. He says there are many fish in the river which runs near the house (the Avon).

∽ *Tuesday 7 August.* Mr Spencer is the village apothecary. They say he is very capable although he is quite young. Lady Glengall came to lunch. She is going to Caher, her property in Ireland. She had left behind her two daughters, Lady Charlotte and Lady Emily Butler, with Mr Brooke Greville, who is their chevalier on this journey.

∽ *Wednesday 8 August.* The ladies went to Chippenham this evening. I read Cooper's 'The Pilot'.

∽ *Thursday 9 August 1827.* Went this evening to Melksham, a little town three miles from here with a pleasant situation. This morning we heard of the death of Mr

Canning with the regrets that one can only feel but cannot express. He was the hope for universal freedom. He died of an inflammation of the liver, yesterday, Wednesday August 8th, at 4 in the morning, at Chiswick, the villa of the Duke of Devonshire, near London, in the same room where the great Fox had died earlier, who had been, in the same way as Mr Canning, invited by the late Duke of Devonshire to recover his health. They say that Mrs Canning has completely lost her reason. This statesman's death must be deeply felt by all those who have any spark of generous feeling. Everyone is wondering what will happen next. The Apostolics will acclaim victory and the Constitution of Portugal is practically dead.

∞ *Friday 10 August.* The poet Thomas Moore came this morning: he is almost our neighbour, living in a pretty cottage at Sloperton, four miles from here.

∞ *Saturday 11 August.* Heard of the death of the excellent Lady Susan O'Brien, who had twice so kindly received me at Stinsford: I had a presentiment on leaving her that I should never see her again. She was more than 80 years old, having a lively sophisticated wit, very lovable, with old-fashioned courtly manners. She had no infirmities and kept her faculties to the end. They say that, luckily, she had no suffering at all.

∞ *Sunday 12 August.* Went to church. I like the look and the manners of Mr Paley. There are two or three very curious windows in our church; Gothic, of a good style.

∞ *Monday 13 August.* Mr Talbot showed us the Great Charter, Magna Charta conceded by King John to the Barons. This one was given by his son, Henry III, to Ela Countess of Salisbury, who was Sheriff of the County of Wilts in 1226. It is the fundamental basis of English freedom. It is on a well-preserved sheet of parchment, with the seal of Henry III. It is always kept in a room in the tower where the archives are kept. Mr Awdry, the steward of the property, came and opened the muniment room for us.

∞ *Tuesday 14 August.* A tuner came from Devizes to tune the piano, with the excellent

'3 August 1827: Mr. Talbot showed us the Great Charter, Magna Charta, conceded by King John to the Barons.'

harp by Érard, which Mr F. bought before leaving London. It is a perfect instrument; the piano is also very good.

∞ *Wednesday 15 August.* An old Mr Ford, 80 years old, who lives at Pickwick Lodge, quite near here, and Mr Awdry, dined with us.

∞ *Thursday 16 August.* They left for Bath and returned because of the rain. There was a storm. Thunder and lightning.

∞ *Friday 17 August.* Mr and Mrs Methuen, daughter of Lady Mildmay, came to visit, They live at Corsham Court, three miles from here. The ladies went to Bowood, it is only five miles away.

∞ *Saturday 18 August.* The Porter from Bowood came to tune the piano! We found an ancient secret staircase which goes from the East Gallery into the garden and into the cloister. Its doors were walled up. We made endless conjectures on the subject. It was full of bats which put out the light whenever we went in there.

∞ *Sunday 19 August.* Lady E. was with Mrs Methuen at Corsham. Walk to Notton to see Mr Elms's beautiful carnations.

∞ *Monday 20 August.* Three young wandering dandies, Mr Eden, Mr Glyn and Mr Hamilton, came to visit the Abbey in the pouring rain. We gave them hospitality. A very curious old dress of embroidered red satin was found.

∞ *Tuesday 21 August.* We all went shopping in Bath in the sociable. The weather was beautiful. We crossed a charming countryside on the way there, very undulating, well cultivated and thickly populated. I had already gone to Bath from Clifton two years ago: it is a charming town. We came back to dinner at the Abbey at 9 pm.

∞ *Wednesday 22 August.* Mr William Strangways came from London. Mr John and Mrs Awdry came to visit us. Lord Kerry and his tutor, Mr Guthrie, came to dinner from Bowood. We were all very gay, toured all the house. There are stables called after Cromwell because they say he put his horses there after taking the Abbey in the Rebellion. We went in the tower, and on the top of it. This tower has a room on the ground floor, one on the floor above for the archives, one on the second floor which will make an excellent observatory and a platform on the third floor, from which there is an extensive view. It is called Elizabeth's Tower, because they say it was built in her time. There is an old tradition that Queen Elizabeth spent a night at the Abbey on one of her journeys.

∞ *Thursday 23 August.* Horatia's birthday. She is 18. She received some nice presents. Mr Moore the poet came from Sloperton to dinner with us. He was gay, amiable, and sparkling with wit. The dinner was very merry. We took him on a tour of the house and accompanied him on Bowden Hill with Mr W. St. and all the family.

∞ Friday 24 August. Lady Louisa Fitzmaurice came on horseback from Bowood. We all went to Bowood in the evening in the sociable. Saw the garden, where there are charming flowers, an Italian terrace, a superb house, a beautiful park. I had practically forgotten all that, not having been there for 7 years: we walked a long time in the beautiful park, where we met Lord Kerry, Lady Louisa, little Marie, her French

Bust of the poet Thomas Moore, now in the possession of the Bath Royal Literary and Scientific Institution

companion, little Lord Henry Fitzmaurice and Mr Guthrie. Mr W. Strangways talked to us much about Russia on our return.

Saturday 25 August. Mr W. Strangways left at 6 this morning for Melbury, where he is going to join his mother, Lady Ilchester. Mr Harisson, the architect, arrived. We were amused to examine the secret staircase with him. A hole has been made into the Gallery. We must unblock the door to make a passage into the garden.

Sunday 26 August. Went to church. Excellent sermon from Mr Paley on drunkenness, because on making his rounds late yesterday evening, he had found all our servants drowning their sorrows in numerous pots of beer in a little tavern in the village. Mr Paley is truly that which all good priests who do their duty ought to be. Mr Harisson left for Carclew in Cornwall to Sir Charles Lemon. We all went in the calèche to Sloperton, near Bromham, the cottage of Anacreon Moore whom we met on the way, walking and reading, dreaming of the sound of lyre and verse. He climbed into the carriage with us and came as far as Mrs Dickinson's, whose beautiful park, covering the hillside, he had crossed. He showed us a caricature which represents Walter Scott and Mr Moore in a balance. The Scotsman is sitting the higher, sadly regarding his nine heavy volumes of *Napoleon* piled on his knees, while the little Moore, who weighs down the scales, holds his small volume, the *Epicurean*, triumphantly in the air. A charming piece of work, full of interest.

Monday 27 August. In the evening they all went to Pickwick Lodge, to Mrs Ford. They are old childhood friends of Lady Elisabeth's. I walked alone in the meadow, sat beside the river Avon and read several of Ovid's letters in English.

Tuesday 28 August. Went shopping in Chippenham. There is hardly anything in the shops. Chippenham is a pretty little town, which sends a member to the House of Commons. Mr Grosset is the member for this town. The countryside between Laycock and Chippenham is very agreeable. We met Mr Feilding on horseback and little Morphine. Mr Talbot on the other hand went to Castle Combe to see his friend Mr Scroop. He had the misfortune to take a toss from his horse while he was returning at night. He fell on his head and hurt himself quite considerably, however there was nothing very serious in this accident.

Wednesday 29 August. We walked a lot today in the fields, near the waterfall, along the river, and this evening we went to Ray Bridge a little hamlet half a mile from here, where there is a pretty little house which belongs to Mr T., which I call my cottage because I would very much like it to be mine. There is a little tower which can be seen from the Abbey. We toured the village and its little streets. We played music in the evening. Excellent harp. Piano out of tune. Old Mr Ford came this morning. He has recovered after being seriously ill. Mr Talbot is better this evening. He stayed in his room all day. Mr Spencer does not wish to bleed him, he will pull through without that.

I wrote a few lines to Mr Montgomerie, who is at his house at Garboldisham in Norfolk, where he also is making repairs.

Thursday 30 August. Lord Kerry came from Bowood to fish in the Avon. We fished for two hours without catching anything. The wind was quite sharp. He brought his dinner in a basket, and ate it beside the water.

It seems that the Ministry is tottering. The Whigs don't wish Mr Herries for Chancellor of the Exchequer. Mr Huskisson is returning from Paris. It is feared that the King will not appoint him. Lord Goderich does not seem to have the stature for the position; it needs another man to replace Mr Canning! The Duke of Wellington has resumed his position of Commander in Chief. The star of the Whigs seems to be fading. Lord Lansdowne is expected at Bowood, which proves that he does not adhere to the new arrangements, which would not be based on liberal principles, and that the ministry will doubtless dissolve itself of its own accord, which is deeply to be regretted for the party properly thinking of the human race!... Mr Talbot does not seem very well today.

Friday 31. Went to Innwood two miles from here. It is a pretty wood which belongs to Mr Talbot. He is better today and came with us. Went to Beanacre. Mrs and Miss Ford came this morning. (Read the memoirs on the Consulate). Beautiful weather.

Saturday 1st September. Went to Sloperton cottage to see the poet Moore. It is a charming retreat, which accords with the spirit of its owner, simple, agreeable, and with a lighthearted manner like his imagination.

Monday 3 September. The young ladies went to Bowood with their papa. Milady stayed here to look after Mr Talbot. At Bowood there were Mr and Mrs Barton, daughter of the English consul at Bordeaux, who is very pretty, Mr Moore, Mrs and Mr Bowles, the poet.

Thursday 6 September. All the family returned from Bowood, with Milady, who went there yesterday for dinner. Mr F. stayed there to see Mr and Mrs Heneage one of the beauties of Wiltshire.

◌ *Friday 7.* Visits all day. Mr and Mrs Scroop from Castle Combe; Mrs Houlton and one of her daughters from Farley Castle. Sir Charles Lemon came to stay for several days.

◌ *Saturday 8.* Endless visits. Among others, Lady Lansdowne with Mr and Mrs Anisson, who is the sister of Mrs de Barente. She is ugly and quite insignificant in conversation. They have come to make a tour of England.

◌ *Sunday 9.* They went to dine at Bowood in pouring rain which never stopped all day. Caroline stayed at home. Mr and Mrs Anisson were still at Bowood. I read Antommarchi's work, (*The Last Moments of Napoleon*). [...] My brother Ferdinand was still in Rio Janiero on the 2nd June. [...]

◌ *Monday 10.* The King of France went to the camp of St. Omer ostensibly to make a review, but in fact to fulfil a vow which he made to Notre Dame de Liesse. He was at Cambray on the 7th. They talk still of a law on the press. The censorship leaves too much freedom according to the Jesuits. The famous Deputy, Manuel, is dead. There were still scandals at his funeral, the police having wished to prevent the friends of the dead man from carrying his coffin on their shoulders. The English Ministry has finally been arranged: with Lord Goderich (formerly Mr Robinson) as Prime Minister and First Lord of the Treasury, Lord Lansdowne has consented to keep the portfolio of the Interior, Lord Dudley Ward that of Foreign Affairs, Mr Herries has been made Chancellor of the Exchequer; they say that he is a very pronounced Tory. How will all these different elements work together! Mr Canning's death is a great loss! However, one hopes that the Ministry, which is partly composed of those whom he had chosen, will not depart from the principles he had adopted for the good fortune and freedom of the people. It is said that the Emperor Don Pedro has named his brother Don Miguel Regent of Portugal. If that is true, the English have no choice but to withdraw their troops; thus the Jesuits and the Apostolics would have again won in that matter.

◌ *Tuesday 11 September.* Mr Talbot discovered among the ancient papers kept in the tower two large parchment books containing the gifts made to the convent and some ancient accounts, among which there is a very curious mention of the amount of bread, beef, mutton, veal, eggs, pigeons, pigs, vegetables, grain, fruits and wine which was consumed annually. Much of it is in old French, but most in Latin going back as far as the reign of Richard II and even of John. Sir Charles Lemon left for Bowood.

◌ *Wednesday 12 September.* They all went to dinner at Bowood except Horatia.

◌ *Thursday 13.* In digging up the floor of the old chapter house to make a water course the workmen found an uncovered stone coffin containing bones. They were exhumed, and some teeth were found, of a perfect whiteness and very well preserved,

◌ *Friday 14.* Lord Lansdowne came with the Hon. William Fox Strangways who came to spend a day with his family to make his farewells. Lord Lansdowne appeared in very good spirits, he was shown the house. We deciphered some of the ancient papers.

Lord Lansdowne, 3rd Marquess (1780–1863), Whig statesman and landowner

Napoleon Bonaparte (1769–1821). '25 June 1826: Horatia gave me today a beautiful engraving of Napoleon's portrait.'

Saturday 15. A pleasant walk to Nash Hill, where Mr Talbot has a farm. We were accosted by an old village woman called Anne Pierce. She was formerly a domestic servant in the abbey. She asked us to have her little grand-daughter admitted to the school.

Sunday 16. Went to church. Moderate sermon. Walk to Raybridge. Mr W. Strangways left us this morning for Florence. Mr Talbot accompanies him as far as London.

Monday 17. We made a very agreeable excursion to Draycot. The house has a very undistinguished exterior, but is in the middle of a magnificent park. We found there Lord and Lady Lansdowne and their children, Lord Kerry, little Lord Henry Fitzmaurice, Lady Louisa Fitzmaurice, little Mary, and Mr Guthrie, whom Lady Elisabeth had arranged to meet. We visited the house, which is not pretty. The rooms are small low and dull, and after having toured the park, as much on foot as in the carriage, we sat on a slope where we looked over an extended and varied view and we had an excellent lunch on the grass. Lady Lansdowne was charged with bringing the food and acquitted herself marvellously. We all had a great fount of gaiety, excited by the air and by the charming sights which surrounded us. We did justice to the lunch and then went to visit the church, where there is a curious tomb of a knight. He is lying on a low stone with his legs crossed according to the custom of the times to show that he had been on a Crusade. Hanging on the wall were spurs, a helmet, a standard, a coat of mail and a pair of gauntlets. The coat of arms of Mrs Long Wellesley is placed among those of her family. It is there that she was taken prematurely by a very poignant grief, caused by her husband, whose conduct was unworthy. Draycot belonged to the Long family. Sir Tilney Long left it to his eldest daughter Mrs Long Wellesley, together with Wanstead and several other possessions, so that she enjoyed some £40,000 in revenue, which her husband found means of dissipating. Draycot belongs now to her eldest son under the guardianship of a tutor. We returned to the Abbey, very tired, at 6.30.

Tuesday 18 Sept. We were very tired after cleaning the portraits of Mr Talbot's ancestors which we have arranged in the East Gallery. Mr Montgomerie arrived this evening from Garboldisham.

Wednesday 19. I went to Bath with Mr F. to buy strings for the harp. This town seems to be declining and there is little to buy. We had great difficulty in getting what we needed. It was very cold, but fine. Morphine ran all the way coming and going, at least 26 miles. I was very tired.

Thursday 20. The architect, Mr Harisson, came. Lady Elisabeth and Horatia went to visit Lady Mildmay and Letitia who are at Corsham with Mrs Methuen, daughter of Lady Mildmay.

Friday 21. Lord and Lady Lansdowne and Mr Th. Moore came to dinner in terrible weather. Lady Lansdowne was very indisposed during dinner. Lord Lansdowne was preoccupied. The amiable poet alone enlivened the conversation. He slept at the house. We played much music in the evening, playing the piano and the harp and singing.

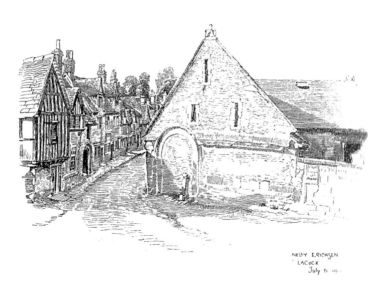

NELLY ERICHSEN
LACOCK
July 31 19..

⌒ *Saturday 22 September.* Mr Moore sang us several of his new songs, entitled *Evenings
in Greece.* He is now occupied in writing the life of Lord Byron. Walk to Spye-Park
the home of Mr Starkey.

⌒ *Tuesday 25.* The newspapers announce a complaint from the Greek leaders who
were commanding in the Acropolis at Athens at the time of the capitulation, a
complaint directed against the brave Colonel Fabrier, who, according to them, be-
trayed the cause of Greek freedom by his intrigues with Admiral Rigny, and caused
the surrender of the citadel, although it still had five months' provisions. One does
not know what to make of all that. It is not the first example of ingratitude on
the part of the Greeks. They have demanded that he should be judged by a court
martial. Doubtless he will be sacrificed. It will be the reward of his devotion, and
of his blood spilled in the cause of the perfidious Hellenes!

Last Saturday's *Globe* carried in full a letter from Sir Walter Scott, together with
documents taken from Foreign Office correspondence, in refutation of General
Gourgand's letter which denied several assertions injurious for the reputation of that
general which had been advanced, among a great number of falsehoods, in the life
of Napoleon published by W. Scott, in which he has not maintained his reputation
as a great writer. It is a tissue of incoherences, of facts which are invented or taken
from the lampoons of the time. In fact it proves that he knew neither the men, nor
the things, nor the times of which he was writing, and that the prejudices usually
attached to ignorance dictated this heavy work in nine volumes. The conduct which
he attributed to General Gourgand was that of the vilest of men; however it must
be admitted that the Scotsman, for his part, produced letters taken from the Foreign
Office, where this personage seems to play a double role which will make him hate-
ful to posterity, and odious to every honest man, if he does not succeed in proving
clearly that he has been libelled. (Went to Bowood, visited the park and the house).

Thursday 27 September. Pouring rain. We waited at breakfast for Mrs Money, whom Lady E. had known in Paris. She is one of the Bourbels, married to a Mr Money, English resident in Calcutta. Mrs Money's health having suffered in the climate of India, she has come to Europe to recover. She has six children. She has only been in England for a few days, where she has come to see two of her brothers-in-law. One of them lives near here at Wetham whence she comes at the moment, and she is going to stay with the other in Herefordshire. Her mother was English, which means that she speaks English almost like a native; it is true that she was brought up in this country, as an émigrée, together with her brother, M. de Bourbel, whom we knew in Paris last winter. In Paris Mrs Money lives in the same house as Mme de Montholon, and it is through her that Lady E. met General de Montholon and the Countess. She arrived at 11 o'clock, after we had had breakfast. She had two of her little boys with her. She is not nearly so pretty as we had been told; we are in the land of exaggeration, that is my opinion.

Friday 28. Visit to the Miss Awdrys of Notton.

Saturday 29. The ladies went to dinner with Mrs Methuen at Corsham. Milady had a bad pain in her face; she did not go out.

Sunday 30. Went to church. Mr Money from Wetham preached in Mr Paley's absence. He is more lively than most Protestant preachers. He preached about plenty with a tone of conviction which made an impression – he came to have his lunch with us, as well as the three Misses Awdry, whom we had invited. Afterwards we went to the village school. Each of these ladies teaches a class of these poor children.

Monday 1st October. Walk to Notton, Lackham etc. Bought pinks from Mr Elms.

Tuesday 2 October. We gardened for two hours. We planted double primulas and polyanthus, pinks and hyacinth bulbs.

Wednesday 3 October. Lady Mildmay and Letitia came from Corsham to visit us, with Mrs Methuen, who has been in the fashion this year in London, although there is nothing remarkable about her, but she is very pretentious. Letitia is very dressed-up for the country.

Thursday 4. Great sorrow, we found our gardens laid waste by horses and cows which came in through the shrubbery and made great havoc: the cows ate six pinks. Walk to Bowden Hill to see a poor family (Mary Barnes).

Saturday 5 October. Walk to Bowden Hill and to Nash Hill, from where one enjoys a magnificent view. Went to Nethermoor Farm, which belongs to Mr Talbot. We were received there by the farmer's wife, who is that which all farmer's wives ought to be, a good housekeeper who never plays the harp and never reads Ariosto but herself feeds the numerous inhabitants of the farmyard and is in charge of all the details of the farm. Her daughter, a very fresh young peasant girl, was occupied milking the cows. She offered us a glass of excellent warm milk which Caroline and Horatia accepted. We were made to sit down in a very clean small room near the kitchen, where comfort was not lacking, although it was easy to see that everything in this house was devoted to utility and to a well arranged economy. This farm is very isolated, situated on the slope of the hill. The family of this honest farmer, Mr Croker, has been established in this county for 600 years and in this farm for half that time.

Saturday 13. All the family went to Bowood. I spent the time re-reading the memoirs of M. Henry de Chaboulon, which are very well written and extremely interesting. I started to put down on paper some fragments of memoirs about myself: I don't think I shall continue. They could only be for me; I know no-one to whom I should like to show them. This week we have entertained ourselves by reading the comedies, *La Coquette Corrigée* by Delanoue, the *Philinte de Molière* by Fabre d'Eglantine, *Le Misanthrope* by Molière. The *Baruffe Chiozotte*, a comedy by Goldoni, very amusing in Venetian dialect, which is full of freshness and grace.

Monday 15. Lady à Court came to stay for several days. She has been Ambassador's wife in Naples, in Madrid and in Lisbon, where her husband, Sir William à Court, still is. She speaks all these languages, as well as English and French, with great ease. She has very distinguished manners, and is very agreeable in company because she has seen much and travelled so much. She has been to Tunis, to Algiers and to Tangier etc. We played much music. Lady à Court sings Spanish and Portuguese songs.

Wednesday 17. Lady à Court sang all the morning. Her daughter Cécile is with her. She does not appear to have inherited her mother's talents.

Friday 19. Lady à Court and her daughter left for Bowood. We walked through the fields with Mr Feilding to see a wool spinning-mill with machinery set in motion by a water-mill.

Saturday 20 October. It is six years ago today that we crossed Mount Cenis to enter Italy. I went with the ladies to Calne, which is 7 miles from here, to see a Nursery Garden. [...]

Tuesday 23 October. All the family left for Bowood. I read *The Prairie*, a novel by the American, Cooper.

Friday 26 October. All the family returned from Bowood.

Saturday 27. Worked for a long time in the garden, planted rose bushes, tulips and hyacinths. We had a visit from everybody at Bowood, Lord and Lady Lansdowne, Mr and Mrs Fazakerly whom I had not seen since Nice and whom I was very pleased to see again. Mr Fazakerly says that he never believed I could have enjoyed myself at Lacock. There was also Mr Baillie, whom I knew at Richmond, Mr and Mrs Cunliffe, Mr Murray and Mr Romilly, the eldest son of Sir Samuel Romilly; he has returned from Greece. We toured the cloisters, the house and the gardens with them.

Monday 29 October. They all went to dine at Compton Basset with Mr and Mrs Heneage. Mr T Moore was there, the Rev. Mr Bowles etc, etc. I stayed behind with Horatia. We read one act of the *Villeggiatura*.

Tuesday 30. Mr and Mrs Nicholl came to dine with their three pretty children, Johny, Lucy and Christina.

Wednesday 31. The Marquess of Lansdowne came to see Mrs Nicholl with his daughter Lady Louisa Fitzmaurice. Mr and Mrs Nicholl left after lunch for London.

🕮 *Thursday 1st November.* Mr Moore came to dine and to stay the night; but when he learned that Mr F. and Lady E. had gone to Bath for the day he didn't want to stay. We planted in the garden some flowers that came from Bowood.

🕮 *Friday 2 November.* We met a man on a lonely path who demanded alms from us, and whose disordered appearance alarmed us. He spoke in a vague manner, interrupted with mystical phrases, normally used by the Methodists. We sent him to the Abbey to get rid of him. We went to visit poor people, among others Joseph Humphries, an old man 80 years old, at Beaulieu Common. He was surrounded by his grandchildren and by his daughter-in-law. Saw also Mrs Showering, sister-in-law of Mary Barnes and mother of Joseph Humphries's daughter-in-law (Succhy Hunt).

🕮 *Saturday 3 November.* Played whist. I won with Lady E.

🕮 *Monday 5 November.* Went to see Daniel Robins, the poor mason who has fallen from some scaffolding. Nothing is broken. Walked as far as Mary Barnes's cottage.

🕮 *Tuesday 6 November.* Lady Mary, Sir Christopher Cole and the Misses Isabella and Emma Talbot arrived for dinner. We played music in the evening and looked at Emma's pretty drawings. Walk to Bowden Hill.

🕮 *Wednesday 7.* Lady Mary Cole, Sir Christopher and their family left after lunch. Emma sketched various views of the house and of the church. Beautiful weather. Walk with Mr F. to Nash Hill. We surprised a poacher hunting in a little wood belonging to Mr Talbot. He jumped a hedge and a ditch, ran away from us as fast as his legs would go, and threw his gun behind a bush. Then he had the impudence to come back to us to claim his dog, which we were trying to catch. Mr F. discovered later that he is a tanner from Chippenham who is known in the neighbourhood as a poacher.

🕮 *Thursday 8.* We had for dinner Mr Moore, Lord Auckland and his sister Miss Eden, who had both returned from Ireland. Miss Eden has lived much in society, she is very witty and draws marvellously, especially figures. She says that Irish poverty is at its height.

🕮 *Friday 9 November.* Miss Eden, Lord Auckland and Mr Moore left after breakfast. All last evening Mr Moore sang the most graceful melodies. He was very gay.

🕮 *Saturday 10.* Planted in the little gardens a single rosebush, a noisette rosebush and some narcissi. Copied some music for our amiable poet. Played whist in the evening. Won.

🕮 *Sunday 11.* Mr Feilding left for Sandleford Priory to stay with Miss Montaigu. The newspaper brought the news of the brilliant victory of Navarino gained over the Turks and Egyptians of Ibrahim Pasha by the combined English, French and Russian fleets under the command of Admiral Sir Edward Codrington, Admiral de Rigny and Count Heiden. Twenty-five ships had destroyed more than two hundred Turks. Ibrahim had violated the armistice in continuing his atrocities against the Greeks. It is said that several Austrian ships were destroyed carrying Turkish flags. What a disgrace! This battle took place in the Gulf of Navarino on the 20th October last (Saturday, 1827), lasting from 3 o'clock in the afternoon until 7 p.m. Unfortunately there were many killed and wounded and our ships were badly damaged. We wait impatiently for more news.

Monday 12. Details of the Battle of Navarino.

Tuesday 13. Went to Sloperton to see our poet, whose doors were all locked. All the family were out. Toured the pretty village of Bromham, near Sloperton. Visited Mrs Napier who has several pretty children. The smallest, called Pamela, is charming. Two of the children are unfortunately deaf and dumb. Mrs Napier is the daughter of General Fox, brother of the famous Fox: and her husband the son of beautiful Lady Sarah Bunbury who later married a Mr Napier. This man is a Colonel and has written about the war in Spain, in which he took part. He is said to be very talented.

Wednesday 14. Gloomy weather. Much rain. The King and Villèle have just made seventy-six peers, including M. Frenilly, M. Olivier etc. and others of the same sort!! They have revoked the censorship until the 5th of February next, the day of the opening of Parliament: they are doing dreadful things as ministers, recounted by the papers, from which the chains have been removed.

Thursday 15. The Rev. Mr Bowles came to visit us. He is a poet, a wit, a canon of Salisbury Cathedral; but a very good man and an original. He lives at Bremhill, 7 miles from here.

Friday 16. Walk to Sandy Lane. We have a flood. The Avon has come out of its banks, and we seem to be in the middle of a lake. Visited a poor woman who made me cry by telling me of the recent death of one of her daughters-in-law.

Saturday 17. Mr Talbot has left for Pixton in Devonshire to stay with Lord Carnarvon. The river has risen further. Giovannina said on seeing it, "diventeremo pesci d'acqua dolce"!! [we are going to turn into fresh-water fish]

Sunday 18. Sermon from Mr Paley on hypocrisy. Beware the leaven of the Pharisees, which is hypocrisy. St. Luke, ch. 12, v.1.

Tuesday 20. Mr F. arrived from London. He did not bring much news, but it appears that not everbody agrees that it was necessary for Admiral Codrington to fight.

Wednesday 21 November. Beautiful weather. Walk to the house of Spye Park. Met the poet Moore in the fields. He is always full of gaiety. He maintains that women have less physical feeling than men, and for that reason, he says, they are better able to bear pain. He says also that women and priests are cruel because they are equally feeble and cowardly.

Thursday. Very cold. We have heard of several thefts in the neighbourhood, which lessens my fondness for the people of Laycock.

Friday 23. Very cold. Snow. The King of France has named M. de Rigny Vice-Admiral (he was Rear-Admiral), and Captain Milins Rear-Admiral. The Captains who have distinguished themselves have been decorated, as well as Admiral Codrington and Admiral Heyden, who have received the Grande Croix de St. Louis. Captain

Fellowes has been given the Order of the Legion of Honour, and the brave Captain Hugon only the Legion of Honour like the others.

Paris has elected her eight Deputies. They are all very good Liberals: Casimir Perrier, Benjamin Constant, Dupont de l'Eure, M. Jacques Lafitte, M. Fernaux, Royer-Collard, M. Schönen and Baron Louis. They say this trend will be followed in the whole of France, and everything leads one to believe that the Ministry has no reason to be pleased at having risked the test of dissolving the Chamber in order to find some more manageable instruments. A necessary change in the Ministry is spoken of. They announce censorship for the 30th of this month, before the electors of Corsica have had time to come together, seeing that their transactions do not begin until the 5th of January!

It seems that here, as there, the victory of Navarino is rather embarrassing. Some say that the Admirals have overstepped their powers. One waits with apprehension for news from Constantinople and the unlucky Franks exposed to the vengeance of the Turks. On the 25th October it was still peaceful in that capital.

Saturday 24 November. Long walk with Mr F. in the snow, with a brilliant sun. Walked to Bowden Hill. Mr Talbot returned from Pixton (Lord Carnarvon's), where he had the bad luck to be overturned, through the clumsiness of the postilion. He was not hurt, but poor Giovanni was less lucky; he was thrown below the coach box and the postilion fell on top of him. He suffers much. He was treated by acupuncture, which is much more painful and quite useless for bruises.

Sunday 25. Thaw. Damp. Cold and disagreeable weather. I went to church with Mr F. without the young ladies.

Monday 26. We met Mr F. hunting in a field with Cattle the gamekeeper. We went with him, but he had no luck. He killed only one woodcock. The weather was beautiful, only too hot. Morphine was horribly afraid of the gun, poor little thing. One day in Salzburg she was on the point of throwing herself out of the window on hearing the cannon fire.

We visited some poor people on the hill.

Tuesday 27. Visited the poor families on Bowden Hill. Milady gave woollen blankets to some, flannel petticoats and waistcoats to others. We make little dresses for the children.

Wednesday 28. Beautiful light effects in the cloisters at sunset. We walked in the Nuns' Kitchen, the Vestry, the Chapter House etc. Mr Bowles, the clergyman from Bremhill, came to dinner with his wife and Mr Moore, who was, as always, full of gaiety and wit. Mr Bowles is a poet, and he has plenty of originality; also he is a very good man. We played music in the evening.

Thursday 29. Mr and Mrs Bowles and Mr Moore left after luncheon. Mr Bowles had received a letter warning him of a resolution passed by the magistrates of Devizes which would prevent him from visiting that unfortunate housekeeper whom they have had the inhumanity to condemn to prison for 2 years and in solitary confinement, and all for having stolen an old tea-pot worth 7 shillings. He left immediately to deal with this affair. He has written a petition to the

King asking his Majesty to commute a punishment so unjustly inflicted. Lord Lansdowne is to present the petition.

⟲ *Sunday 2 December.* I did not go to church. [...] Lord Auckland arrived from London to dinner. He brought me two letters. [...]

⟲ *Monday 3.* Lord Auckland and Mr Feilding left for Redlynch to hunt with Lord Ilchester. Walked to Bowden Hill and visited poor people.

⟲ *Tuesday 4.* Walk in the village. Stormy weather. Milady has had some holly-trees planted. Boatswain is lost; he is a huge dog, our guard and companion on our walks.

⟲ *Thursday 6.* Lord Carnarvon, his daughter Lady Henrietta Herbert, with whom I stayed for several days at Highclere at the end of the winter of 1820, and Mr Moore came to dine. The latter sang much in the evening. Lord Carnarvon was silent throughout dinner.

⟲ *Friday 7 December.* Mr Moore played much music. He sang old English, Irish and Scottish melodies. We had to leave at 2 o'clock, as he was dining with Dr Starky.
Mr and Mrs Scroop came to dinner. He is a college friend of Mr Talbot's. He has studied the geology of the Auvergne and has written a most interesting book about it. He has travelled a lot. Mrs Scroop is a very pleasant young lady.

⟲ *Saturday 8 December.* Lord Carnarvon, Lady Henrietta Herbert, Mr & Mrs Scroop all left after lunch. It was beautiful weather. Mr Feilding and Lord Auckland arrived from Redlynch at 11.30 p.m: after our whist.

⟲ *Sunday 9 December.* Our ambassadors are again in Constantinople. The Turks have shown fresh moderation at the news of the destruction of their fleet at Navarino. Nothing has yet been decided.
Most of the election results in France are liberal, this is a coup which the Government could hardly have expected. [...] It cannot withstand such an opposition. The electors and the sane majority of the nation applaud from one end of France to the other. There were popular risings in Paris on the 19th, 20th and 21st and 22nd of November; the police having wished to oppose gatherings of people who rejoiced at the liberal elections and wished to set fire to the house of those who were known to profess contrary opinions – the soldiers of the line, the gendarmerie, and even the Royal Guard fired on the people. There were 20 people killed and 150 wounded.

⟲ *Sunday 9 December.* Terrible weather. Lord Auckland stayed with us all day.

⟲ *Monday 10 December.* Lord Auckland left this morning for London. Mrs Napier from Bromham came to dine with us. Colonel Napier, her husband, is very busy writing the history of the Peninsular War, which prevented him from coming too. Mr and Mrs Moore were of the party. She has been very beautiful. She still has very regular features and a good figure, very stiff. However very bad health and cares have spoilt her beauty more than they should have done. She is very shy and silent and does not much enjoy company. Her husband loves her tenderly and it is a very happy household. She is a marvel of sweetness, [some people change!] evenness, economy and activity in her house, which is far from rich in spite of

S. Cyriac, Lacock —West.

her husband's hard work and good reputation. We played much music; I played on the harp the duet from the *Barber of Seville*, the one from the *Donna del Lago* with Horatia, and sang with the poet Mozart's *Deh! prendi un dolce amplesso*, from the *Clemenza di Tito*. We tried next some fragments of that admirable! three times admirable!!! *Requiem* of Mozart. He sang a melody, the *Evening Gun*, full of poetry and sentiment. He is always amiable.

Tuesday 11. Appalling weather. A hurricane. Our company was so gay all the morning! They left after luncheon. All the evening I sang the magnificent and never enough admired *Requiem* and the *Clemenza di Tito*, both worthy to find themselves among the greatest masterpieces.

The King has commuted the punishment of the poor woman in Devizes, according to Mr Bowles's petition, which was presented by Lord Lansdowne. She was to have been transported, after two years of solitary confinement. Mr Bowles has won his case. He has prevailed over the little schemes of the tyrannical Devizes magistrates! These have been laid bare!

Monday 17 December. Mr F. left for Middleton to see Lord Jersey.

Tuesday 18. [...] I have decided to leave soon for Paris. A delay of one year would serve no purpose.

Wednesday 19. It was odious weather, dampness, rain, flooding. We have had this every day for a fortnight. We were busy arranging in a cupboard, which we have called the Museum, all the curiosities which we have collected on our travels. There is a little of everything. Giovannina has been very ill since the day before yesterday. Mr Talbot returned from the Grange, where he stayed with Mr Baring.

Thursday 20 December 1827. It was four years ago today that we were in Genoa and found in the Piazza di Fontana Amorosa our charming little Morphine, whom I love so much. I planted today (at Lacock Abbey) in the corner of the East Terrace, near the square pond, three trees, to leave for these dear children a memorial of our friendship and companionship for nearly eight years. In the middle is a fir-tree, of the species called here Balm of Gilead fir for Caroline, on the left of that an ilex for Horatia and on the right a cedar, of the species called 'red cedar' for me. These trees are no more than 2 to 3 feet high. I hope that they will flourish and that the girls will see them covering with their shade the ancient bronze urn which is called the Nuns' Kettle. In forty or fifty years' time they should be magnificent.

Friday 21 December. Received a letter from Middleton from Mr F.; he is not enjoying himself much this time. Lady Jersey has suddenly changed her politics; it is necessary for her always to be with the opposition. Walk and visit to the Misses Awdry at Notton; they are good and simple. I read *Zaïre* aloud to the children and cried while reading those beautiful verses full of nobility and passion.

Saturday 22. Walked to Wyck Lane. Visited the poor. Mr F. came back from Middleton. Played whist.

Sunday 23. Went to church, then to the school to distribute prizes to the poor children, who were very pleased with them.

Monday 24 December 1827. We sang Mozart's *Requiem,* greater than any music already written and, doubtless, than any still to come. [...] What a soul had that prince of music! Sang also part of Handel's *Messiah,* where there are admirable effects. I read *Tartuffe* aloud to them. Some people came and sang carols beneath our windows, Christmas carols.

Tuesday 25 December. Christmas. Went to church. The villagers again came to sing carols. The family went to spend the day at Bowood; they played charades.

Wednesday 26 December. They returned from Bowood.

Thursday 27. Mr Jones, Mr F.'s clerk while he was at sea, came to spend a few days with us. Walk with him to Wyck Lane. I made preparations for my departure.

Friday 28. Walk with Mr Jones to Bowden in extremely muddy weather.

Saturday 29. Mr Montgomerie came from Norfolk: we played whist with Mr Jones. On going to bed, at midnight, we saw from the windows of the East Gallery a huge fire, which a strong wind seemed to encourage further. We passed a very disturbed night, not being able to find out what was in flames, and fearing that it might be some poor cottages.

☞ *Sunday 30.* We have just learnt that it was a rick of corn to which someone had wickedly set fire yesterday evening of which we saw the flames from the Abbey. Some faggots of dry wood and some sulphur were found. They managed to check the fire at 9 o'clock this morning, when the people of the neighbourhood arrived with the only fire engine in the village. We walked there with Mr Jones. Half the rick, which belonged to the farmer, Joyce, had been saved; but what is left is filled with a detestable smell of smoke. I stepped in mud up to my knees near Ray-Bridge. Mr Jones left for Bristol.

☞ *Monday 31 December.* We all went to the ball at Compton Bassett given by Mrs Walker Heneage, 9 miles from here. We went to dress at Bowood, to be nearer the place of the party. Miss Vernon, Miss Fox and Lord John Russell stayed behind at the house; all the rest of the family were at the ball. Mrs Heneage's house is superb, and newly furnished. There were at least 200 people there. Lady Lansdowne, Lord Lansdowne, Lord Kerry, Mr and Mrs Charles Fox, Sir James MacDonell and Lady MacDonell came also. Nothing could be better arranged than that house. The supper, which was splendid, had been prepared by Gunter, who had come from London with all his staff. The band also came from London and was excellent; there were several pleasant people, among others Mrs Smith, the sister of Mrs Heneage, and newly married; she is charming. And two Misses Scott who had been brought up in Bordeaux where their father was Consul. They appeared very French. Mr and Mrs Moore were there. I came back to the Abbey, very tired, with Mr F. and Mr M. [...] The others went to sleep at Bowood.

1828

☞ *Tuesday 1 January 1828.* Lady Lansdowne asked me and Mr Montgomerie to her ball on Thursday.

☞ *Wednesday 2 January.* The ladies came back. They were busy with their costumes for tomorrow.

☞ *Thursday 3 January.* (My little niece, Amélie, was born today in Lima, Peru.) Ball at Bowood. We dressed ourselves there. Horatia wore the dress of a peasant of Lucerne and Caroline a costume from the neighbourhood of Rome, very pretty, both of them. There were not many people at the ball, but it was very gay, we all enjoyed ourselves very much. There was a supper at 2 o'clock, a little chilly as to conversation. Lord Lansdowne was very gay. He danced the English quadrilles and the 'Boulangère' with as much enjoyment as a young man of 20 years who has nothing but dancing on his mind. I danced several times with Mr Moore: little Lord Henry Fitzmaurice was charming, also little Tommy Moore.

☞ *Friday 4.* We are all very tired. Mr Estcourt, whom we had known in London, came to spend several days with us. He showed us the charming views he had painted in Spain and Portugal. There were two or three of the Alhambra and of the Generalife (which is pronounced Heneralif). What delightfully poetical ideas are recalled by the sight alone of those two names.

Saturday 5. Walk to Chippenham in beautiful weather. On our return we found Mr Coventry Starky with his two sisters (their father is the owner of Spy Park) who were making a visit which I was afraid would last the entire day. Their manners are not at all pleasing! Their father is bankrupt and has rented his house to a Mr Gwynne. There is a superb park, where unfortunately Mr Starky's creditors have caused many trees to be cut down to pay his debts. Mr Estcourt was amused by the vulgar manners of the S's. He drew a pretty picture in Lady Elisabeth's album. He is a friendly, witty, polite young man, a thing which is very rare nowadays. He has learning and talents without the affectation of the young men of the world. [...] He was at Harrow with Mr Talbot. We played at whist. I have made great progress at it.

Sunday 6 January 1828. Went to church. Sad and heavy sermon from Mr Paley on a text from St Luke, Chapter 3. Blessed is the Lord God of Israel who has visited and redeemed his people etc. Mr Moore came to dinner with us. He was very amiable, as he usually is. He sang two of his songs and with me several parts of Mozart's admirable *Requiem*. Mr Estcourt was drawing and listening to the music.

Monday 7 January. We went with Mr Moore to see the cottage at Ray-Bridge in the hope that it could be made habitable if he is obliged to leave Sloperton which is almost in ruins; but he said that the sitting room is too small, that the house is too near the road and that the walks are not so pleasant as those around his cottage at Sloperton. So we have given up the hope of seeing him become our neighbour. We all went to a ball in Chippenham which takes place every year at this time at the Angel Inn; there was nothing very tempting about it. However we were obliged to go to encourage the few amusements which take place in this province where the spirit of bigotry, which goes by the name of Methodism, takes possession of so many minds and fills them with a gloomy fanaticism which condemns balls, comedies and parties which had previously taken place all over England, which they are trying to turn into a Chartreuse. There is nothing very brilliant in Chippenham. The room is large, but it was very badly lit, which made it look depressing. All the society of the neighbourhood was there, but the number of odd provincial characters who filled the place made them *brillar oltre misura* [shine exceedingly]. It was here that I was convinced of the immense superiority of the English nobility over the middle class, which is an excellent example of that which is called vulgar, in the full force of the word, in manners, in appearance etc. – in general with very few exceptions. Lady Lansdowne was there, she looked like a queen! Lord Lansdowne, his son Lord Kerry, Mr Guthrie were there, also Lady Theodosia Hall, sister of Lady de Clifford and the Misses Ricardo. I did not enjoy myself much, except in a conversation with the poet the Reverend Mr Bowles who is full of enthusiasm and gaiety. They served us with tea at midnight. The whole thing was very shabbily done, but there is nothing very surprising in that if one remembers that it was given by the landlady of the Angel who gives the ball and that each person paid only 5s for everything. We returned at two o'clock in the morning. It was shocking weather, piercing cold and damp.

☞ *Tuesday 8 January.* They went to Bowood to see the original drawings of Prout.

☞ *Wednesday 9 January.* Hard frost. We danced and waltzed the whole evening to teach Mr Talbot some figures of the quadrilles. *Miracolo!* [a miracle!]

☞ *Thursday 10.* Walk in Wick Lane. Took clothes to some poor women. One of them asked us for a piece of cloth to wrap up her child which had just died. What horrible poverty! Mr F., Mr M., Mr T. and Mr Moore went to dine with Mr Joy, one of our neighbours who is very pleasant and wishes to creep into Paradise in spite of the saints. Mr Moore came back to sleep here. He appeared bored, with his dinner no doubt?

☞ *Friday 11.* I sang with the amiable poet a duet by Asioli and one by Garcia. We read the *Mercure galant* by Boursault. Waltzed and danced in the evening. I have just read *Vittoria Colonna,* a quite amusing novel about the occupation of Italy by the armies of the French Republic in 1796. I read the *Memoirs of a Contemporary,* or *Memories of a Woman,* a shameless work and a tissue of lies, which is amusing however, because they are people who should interest us and shone on the scene of the world since the end of the last century. I have read the voyage of Captain Head in the pampas. Very interesting, vigorously written, with pace and without pretentiousness. A majestic country still bearing the imprint of creation's sublimity and which the works of man have not spoiled! Civilisation is there in its cradle and does not seem to need to make any great progress?

☞ *Saturday 12th January.* Shocking weather. Impossible to go out. Read aloud Sheridan's pleasant comedy, *The School for Scandal,* which is full of wit and liveliness and which paints, no doubt with a true and faithful brush, the vices of that age. Played whist *al solito il sabato* [as usual on Saturday].

☞ *Sunday 13.* I did not go to church at all. Read the Bible by myself, some of the Psalms of David.

☞ *Monday 14.* Walk along the road to Melksham. Lord Kerry came to learn to waltz with his cousins. Mrs Methuen came to visit us. In the evening I sang with Mr M., and nothing but the *Requiem.* That music possesses a strange magic: if I sing it in the evening. I cannot sleep; I hear all the time the most surprising harmonies. [...]

☞ *Tuesday 15.* Lady Lansdowne came to lunch with us, with Lady Louisa Fitzmaurice, Mary, Lord Kerry, Mr Guthrie and the good little Lord Henry Fitzmaurice. We walked with them in the cloisters, on the tower and all over the house; it was very cold. Mr Talbot returned from staying with Lord Dacre at Woodchester in Gloucestershire. [...]

☞ *Thursday 17 January.* Read the 5th and 6th volumes of *Memoirs of a Contemporary.* Read of the terrible end of Marshal Ney and the disasters at which his wife makes out she had been present.

☞ *Friday 18.* Yesterday we finished Sheridan's witty comedy, *The School for Scandal.* The English Ministry is also nearing dissolution through the weakness of Lord Goderich; it seems that the Duke of Wellington is moving heaven and earth to make his party dominate the new ministry; the High-Church, Tory, anti-national, anti-liberal party. Damp weather. The water is running everywhere on the walls and the woodwork inside our bedrooms.

∞ *Tuesday 22.* Caroline's birthday. Mr Montgomerie made a surprise for her by il-luminating the cloister, which produced the most picturesque effects; the arches stood out in the middle of the ivy, and the light showed up their beautiful carvings. Mr Talbot burnt Bengal candles.

∞ *Wednesday 23.* Mr Frederic Montgomerie arrived this evening; we talked politics and discussed all manner of subjects with him. He is very argumentative.

∞ *Saturday 26.* Played whist with the two Mr Montgomeries.

∞ *Sunday 27.* Mr Frederic Montgomerie left. Walk towards Inwood with the dogs.

∞ *Monday 28.* Left Laycock Abbey at 9 a.m. Dined at Speen Hill. Arrived in London at 9 p.m. I was very cold on the journey.

Amélina went from London to Paris in February 1828, and stayed there with her family until June. When she returned to England, it was to go as compan-ion to the Hopwood family near Manchester, but first she met the Feildings in London, and then accompanied them to Lacock for a few weeks. The account of her journey from France and her few days in London is included to show her ex-periences while travelling, and while enjoying the society and cultural attractions of London – experiences which are typical of her life away from Lacock.

∞ *Monday 9 June.* I embarked this morning at 7.30 in the *Lord Melville*, a steam-packet of 80 horsepower. I found there again my companions from the diligence, and several other agreeable people. The crossing could not have been happier; the sea was quite calm, and the wind, although contrary, was not strong. The tide was also against us, which held us up a little. We arrived at the Tower of London after 8, instead of at 6. On the boat was a very well-educated Portuguese, speaking different languages wonderfully well, an Englishman who seemed to me a well of knowledge, a very good-natured Brazilian, who is going to stay with M Fabayana, General Leharpe, who had brought up the Emperor Alexander, was also to be seen, with a young man from Geneva. The company was delightful and conversa-tion solid and interesting among all these distinguished persons. I was in a state of wonder throughout the whole journey. After our arrival at 8 p.m. I watched for half an hour trying to see Mr F., who I knew should have been awaiting me there, when someone seized me by the arm. I turned round: it was he. He had taken a boat to come and look for me. I took leave of my companions. When I arrived on land, I found my dear Horatia, who had been waiting in the carriage. She dissolved in tears on greeting me. On arrival at Sackville Street I was greeted in the most friendly way possible by Lady E., Caroline, Mr Talbot, Mr Moore, Mr Montgomerie. I found C. and H. rather changed, and above all Mr F. Lady Elisabeth has had a very bad cold for three months, and the children had had whooping cough, which makes them cough a lot still. I was so little tired that I sang until one o'clock in the morning with the poet Moore.

∞ *Tuesday 10 June.* Went to the customs with Mr F. to find my belongings. Came back on the river. Went to see the Panorama of Genoa, where we recognized our house. The sky and sea were admirable. Unpacked all the morning and went to see the rehearsal of *Medea* at the Opera. Nothing could be more extraordinary than to see Mme Pasta, wrapped in half a dozen shawls and coats, hidden by a huge hat with a veil, sitting down practically all the time and limping every time she stood up, hardly able to drag herself along. That is what she is like at rehearsal. In the evening she is a different person; she really is Medea, with all her fury and her cunning. That is real talent.

⬯ *Wednesday 11 June.* Went to the rehearsal of the *Medea* and *La Cenerentola,* where Mlle Sontag showed all her little affectations and the incredible ease of her voice: she is a nightingale. In the evening went to Prince Leopold's box at Covent Garden. Saw *The Point of Honour.* It is only an imitation of *Contumace,* a melodrama of la porte St Martin. Charles Kemble is very handsome in the part of Contumace. He plays it with much feeling and truth. Young played the father – he is a little cold. *The Invincibles* – a farce which has little gaiety and less wit – came next. Mme Vestris appeared in a military costume. She has changed a lot and is no longer at all pretty. Tom and Terry, a pitiful display, of the standard only of *Paradis.*

⬯ *Thursday 12 June.* Mr Moore dined at the house. Sat in the Duke of Devonshire's box at the opera for the benefit of *Curione. Medea* and the second act of *Cenerentola.* Mlle Sontag sang divinely the variations on the air *Nacqui all'affanno* [I was born to suffering].

⬯ *13 Friday.* I was very tired and did not go out.

⬯ *Saturday 14.* Went to the Alien Office with Mr F. to find my passport. Everyone went to Wimbledon to luncheon with the Duke of Somerset except Horatia. I stayed with her. Baron Gavedal came to visit me and asked permission to see me again on our return from Lacock. M. Ferrier d'Epernay came too. Mr Moore lunched with us.

⬯ *Sunday 15.* I found installed here on my arrival Eliza Hunlocke, who has been in England with her mother for six weeks. Lady Hunlocke has gone to Wingerworth, her young son's estate in Derbyshire, to arrange affairs. She has left Charlotte, her elder daughter, in Paris, where I had the pleasure of seeing her often, and where she took me often to the Italian opera. Eliza is left in Lady Elisabeth's care; she is a nice person [...]

⬯ *Monday 16 June.* Lady Elisabeth and Caroline went to lunch with the Duchess of St Albans at Holly Grove. Eliza stayed with us. Milady came home ill.

⬯ *Tuesday 17 June.* We left London after some uncertainty on account of Lady Elisabeth's fever. She lay down in the coach. We stopped at Marlborough, where we had supper and spent the night. There is a very pleasant garden where I walked with Eliza.

⬯ *Wednesday 18 June.* Arrived at Lacock Abbey at one o'clock. It was beautiful weather; the house looked charming as we turned into the drive.

⬯ *Thursday 19.* Went to see the garden, which is in the best condition. The flowers in Caroline's and Horatia's gardens are charming. In the courtyard are delightful little chickens, pheasants and partridges, all newly born and very sweet. Mrs Cattle looks after them like children.

⬯ *Friday 20.* Walked about in the garden.

Engraved by W. Finden

LORD BYRON.
at the age of 19.

'25 June 1828:
**Mr Moore is
much occupied
in writing the
life of his friend
Lord Byron.**'
The engraving
is taken from
Thomas
Moore's *Life of
Byron* (1854)

☙ *Saturday 21.* Rained all day. Did my accounts with Mr F. I wrote to Mrs Hopwood from London. She has not yet answered.

☙ *Sunday 22.* Rain and sunshine alternately. Went to church. Sermon by Mr Paley on humility. In the evening went to Chippenham in the carriage (storm in the morning). I finished Cooper's *Red Rover*, the most interesting character I have yet met in a novel; magical descriptions, original style, but there is a little obscurity in the plot, which is not sufficiently developed. It is in fact a charming work, and the Rover is made to turn all heads.

☙ *Monday 23.* The weather at the moment is unsettled. Cold for the 23rd of June. The evening was very fine and we visited Bowood, which is now in its full magnificence. We walked in the park and we picked many flowers. [...] Mlle Mars is in London with Armand and several actors from the Odéon: she is going to give six performances at the opera. It is said that Charles Kemble will act in a French play with her.

☙ *Tuesday 24 June.* Went to Corsham to see Mr Paul Methuen's beautiful house. The architecture is of Queen Elizabeth's time, restored by Mr Nash. The hall, which is modern, is all in oak, of a fantastic design, a little too fussy. The ground floor room is very large and most imposing. It contains a collection of pictures, on the whole fairly mediocre, but among which I saw the following: *Christ Breaking the Bread* by Carlo Dolci, one of the master's most beautiful faces; a large picture by the same artist shows Mary Magdelene at the Saviour's feet; two landscapes by Salvator Rosa; a magnificent Turk by Rembrandt!!, with an extraordinary effect of light; natural grandeur. A *Madonna* by Carlo Cignani, a sketch by Rubens; a *Descent from the Cross* by the same – a small copy of that beautiful picture now at Antwerp!; a portrait of *Fernand Cortez* by Titian – a pretty landscape by Berghem, a *Christ* by Pordenone; *Masaniello* by Salvator Rosa; two pictures by Guercino – one is *Christ and Nicodemus*, the other the *Samaritan Woman*!

☙ *Wednesday 25 June.* Mr Moore came to dinner with us; he was very talkative. After dinner we accompanied him back to Sloperton. His daughter Anastasia was lying on a sofa enjoying, by the window, the one pleasure that her life of suffering allows her. She has terrible pains in one leg, whose muscles have so far withdrawn that it is now shorter than the other. She is very pleasant, she has a sweet and lively face, with beautiful eyes, pretty teeth, a charming voice and a delightful modesty. She is only fourteen years old, poor little thing, her condition is very distressing. Little Tom has a charming face; he is very like his mother. The youngest of the three, Russell, is not beautiful, but it is said that he has good manners and much wit. Mrs Moore is a pretty and excellent person; she is entirely devoted to her household and to her children. Nothing is more full of laughter than their cottage and the garden surrounding it. It is a true picture of peace and domestic bliss. Mr Moore took us into his Sanctum Sanctorum, which he modestly calls his studio. It is truly the dwelling place of a poet, of a man of the world, of a friend of the arts, or, what is worth more still, of a man with the highest moral qualities as a son, as a father and as a husband. He showed us a chimney clock which he had received from Mlle d'Orléans, together with a letter which does honour both to the princess and to the writer. The subject of the clock is Homer singing to his lyre. A small but no doubt well chosen library is the chief furnishing of this temple of the arts; with some busts of famous men, friends of the poet, their portraits and those of famous artists, a piano which accompanies his melodies, so full of grace and feeling; much music; his father's portrait and that of his mother, to whom he writes twice a week, are hung each side of the mirror above the fireplace, and beneath them are two beautiful medals of Napoleon and Josephine. He sang us an Irish air, full of melancholy and showed us several prints by various talented painters and draughtsmen – his own most lifelike portrait has just been painted by Newton. The prints of statues by Canova, given to him by that remarkable man, with the dedication addressed in his own handwriting. A letter from the Countess Guiccoli, that friend of Lord Byron's, sending him some details he had asked for about that remarkable man; she said that she could not have borne her life after the loss of *nostro divino amico* [our divine friend], as she called him, if she had not had the desire to see his memory avenged by a friend with a talent such as that of Mr Moore. Her letter is well written, very simple and full of feeling; he had received it that very morning, with one from Mr Barry, whom we had known at Genoa. Mr By. had many connections with Lord Byron during his stay in that town. The most noteworthy object is a facsimile of a letter from Lord Byron to Lady Caroline Lamb, at the time of his love for her, a love which some people strongly doubted; which so wounded the vanity of that lady, that she had the extraordinary idea of having a facsimile made of one of his most passionate letters, in which he proposed to run away with her, and of having it circulated in society, so that no-one could ignore it. Mr Moore is much occupied in writing the life of his friend Lord Byron.

Thursday 26. I did not go out: Eliza and Horatia went to Inwood. Mr, Mrs and Miss Awdry came to the Abbey. Mr Paley visited Mr Talbot.

Friday 27. Great heat. Mr Harrison came. We had tea in the garden. I gave Eliza a lecture.

Saturday 28. Left the old abbey with many regrets. Dined at Speenhill; great heat. We found Charlotte Hunlocke in London, who had arrived from Paris the previous evening. I saw her again with great pleasure. I had a letter from Mrs Hopwood, who expects me with her on the 12th July.

Sunday 29 June 1828. Mrs Gwynne came this evening and brought us the sad news of the death of the youngest son of Mr Reading, the Clerk of Works. This young man was drowned yesterday, two hours after our departure from Lacock, while bathing in the Avon, quite near the house. His father and mother are plunged in the deepest grief, also his brother who was with him at the time of the accident. They tried all possible means to revive him, but it was too late; he had been under the water for three quarters of an hour; he could not swim. Three doctors were called but with no success. Everyone is in the deepest consternation.

Amélina remained with the Hopwoods, at their country house near Manchester, from June 1828 until September 1831, but she was able to rejoin the Feilding family for short periods during that time. In December 1828 the Hopwoods decided to take their daughter Mary, who had been ailing for some time, to London for consultation, and Amélina was able to go to Lacock for Christmas.

Thursday 18. Went to Manchester with Mary to the doctors. It has been decided that she will go to London with her mother and I to Lacock.

Friday 19. Packing all day; dreadful weather. Mary a little better.

Saturday 20. The whole family has left for London in appalling weather: Mr Starky stayed with us.

Sunday 21 December. I left at 7 a.m. in Miss Hopwood's coupé. Mr Frank accompanied me, and dealt with the details of my journey with much care. I had said my goodbyes to Miss H. yesterday. The weather quite fine and mild: went through Congleton which has a pleasant situation. Saw from afar Eaton, near Chester, the seat of Lord Grosvenor. Dined at Newcastle-under-Lyme, where I had a letter from Mary and Mrs H. They had slept there yesterday. Mary had stood the journey well. Passed by Stafford. The county of that name is on the whole quite pretty, especially after Lancashire, which is spoilt by its factories. It is deserted. Passed Wolverhampton, a horrible little town, full of machines and furnaces, 10 miles round. The effect produced by these bright fires in the middle of the night is most strange. There are a number of iron foundries. Arrived at Birmingham at 7. Slept at the inn the *Hen and Chickens* (Mrs Waddle), a large house where one is most uncomfortable. Left again in the morning, the 22nd, for Bath. Passed Bromsgrove where there is a pass that is practically Alpine! Lunch at Worcester in an excellent inn, the *Star and Garter*, where I had an excellent lunch and everyone is very polite. The weather was beautiful, and I enjoyed the view of the Malvern Hills for part of the journey, and breathed their delicious air. Passed through Tewkesbury, where I saw a very old church with a beautiful porch. After Gloucester, passed through lovely countryside for twenty miles, to Bath, where I took the post-horses for Laycock and arrived at 11 p.m on the 22 December. I found everyone in good health. Mr F. was not at the Abbey.

23 December. Inspected all the improvements. The Gallery is now very comfortable; they have built a very fine and good fireplace; there are red curtains so that music is screened there and sounds very agreeable. Many of the rooms are furnished very pleasantly; the courtyard is completely cleared and some good coach houses have been built. The south front has the best possible effect; it has been completely remodelled and all the windows in it are beautiful and conform in style to the antiquity of the house.

25 December. Went to church with Lady E., Caroline and Horatia. The villagers came and sang in the cloister and brought in a wassail bowl according to custom. Mr F. is still in Rutlandshire with Lady Caroline Powlett at Somerby, and at Cottesmoor with Lady Eleanor Lowther. We rode on horseback alternately with Mr Montgomerie.

1829

1st January 1829. Lady E. gave me a present of a very pretty pair of amethyst ear-rings, and Caroline gave me the Divino Dante and Horatia a charming little

collection of stories, engravings and poems. Lord Kerry, Lord Henry Fitzmaurice and Mr Colville came from Bowood. We walked to Spye Park.

2 Friday. Walk with Tampon. Horatia went to Bowood where there is a large party.

3 January. Mary Fox and Mrs Vernon-Smith came from Bowood. I went on horseback to Corsham with Mr M. It was very cold and there was a little snow.

5 Monday. Mr Guthrie and little Lord Henry Fitzmaurice came. I tried a horse that Mr F. wanted to buy for Caroline, who rode her own Clotilde, M. and Mme Nérissa. There were six of us on horseback. But my steed was so frisky that it took me to the top of Bowden Hill at a gallop, and so exhausted me when I tried to hold it in that we were obliged to return after having been only as far as the *George Inn.*

Tuesday 6 January. Mr Feilding arrived this morning from London. He brought a new game of Grace, of Waterloo rockets and another game of battledore and shuttlecock – very graceful. Mrs Ord, Miss Fox and Miss Vernon came. Fine weather, frosty.

7 Wednesday. Snow

8 Thursday. Mary Fox, more beautiful than ever, Lady Louisa Fitzmaurice, very much improved, and Mr Fazackerly came from Bowood.

Friday 9 January. Went to a ball at Bowood, where I found all the neighbours from Wiltshire. I met Mr Moore again with great pleasure; Mrs Moore was there also, with her children. Mr Estcourt, who had spent some days with us at the Abbey last year was there also. He was very friendly, his conversation is very varied and very agreeable. Mr Joy found the means to insinuate himself, this year as last. There were also Mr and Mrs Napier, the Misses Ashe, of whom the elder is pleasant, the Starkys, the Moneys, the Riccardos, the youngest is very beautiful. But the beauty of this festivity was without doubt Mary Fox, Lord Holland's daughter; she has an indescribably sweet expression and the best possible manners. The supper was very good but not very lively. Lord Lansdowne was nothing less than healthy. I also saw Mrs Fazackerly again with great pleasure: she is very happy since she is the mother of a three-month-old daughter. Lady Lansdowne was visibly anxious; her eyes hardly left Lord Lansdowne's face.

⚭ *Monday 12 January.* Mr Protheroe, whom I have known in Rome, came to spend some days at the Abbey. He is well-informed and has good manners.

⚭ *Tuesday 13.* Lord Kerry came to dinner.

⚭ *Wednesday 14.* Mr Montgomerie left for Puttenham Priory to stay with his sister. I miss his company. Mr Moore came to dinner and to stay the night here. I sang many of his songs.

⚭ *Thursday 15.* Mr Moore left. Lady E., Mr F., Caroline and Mr Protheroe went to dine and spend the night at Bowood. I stayed behind with Horatia.

⚭ *Friday 16.* Walk to Beanacre with Horatia. Very cold. Wrote to Mrs Hopwood and to Mary. They all came back from Bowood in the evening, the roads were dangerously slippery. Lord Lansdowne has quite recovered.

⚭ *Saturday 17.* Had a letter from Mrs H. which distressed me much; she talks of returning to Hopwood on the 27th. Frost. Walk with Mr F., Caroline and Horatia.

⚭ *Sunday 18 January.* Bad weather. Cold. We didn't go to church.

⚭ *Tuesday 20.* Had a letter from Mrs Hopwood. She has put off her departure until early February, which delights me.

⚭ *Friday 25.* Caroline's birthday. She had nice presents from her father, her mother and her sister.

⚭ *Monday 9 February.* Left Laycock at 7 a.m. with Mr F., who accompanied me in the coupé for 17 miles as far as Cross Hands, where we joined the coach; there was nobody there. I left them with my heart broken. I kissed Caroline and Horatia goodbye in their beds. I am almost of one mind with the man who wrote 'It is more pain to part than pleasure to meet'. The weather was as sad as I was.

During her subsequent lengthy stay at Hopwood Amélina's health declined. She returned to Lacock in September 1831, hoping to make a full recovery there:

⚭ I arrived at Lacock Abbey on Saturday the 10th September 1831 at 10.30 pm. No-one was at home except Mr Talbot, whom I saw again with great pleasure, and most of the servants. They had sent one of their maids from London to look after me, which she did to my perfect satisfaction. With what emotion did I find myself again within the hospitable walls of this old abbey, to which so many interesting memories are attached! I have had such happy times here. [...]

⚭ *11 September.* It was beautiful weather, and as warm as a June day. I crept about in the garden, for that is all I am able to do, to creep about and not to walk. I examined the improvements which had been put into effect during my absence. The new building had been demolished and in its place three large Gothic windows had been added to the South Gallery. One of these bay windows is so large that it makes a kind of drawing room where there are tables, sofas etc. etc. The two others are much smaller; however they form recesses, and in each is a writing table where one can sit very comfortably without being seen by anyone in the Gallery. In fact it

Horatia Feilding, photographed by her half-brother W. H. Fox Talbot

makes a very large, comfortable and artistic room. The ceiling is in very good taste and simple and the windows serve as a pleasant adornment to the outside. The gardens were full of charming rare flowers: above all those of Caroline and Horatia are spangled with the colour of the Maurandia which covered an arbour with its elegant festoons, as well as convolvulus, a pretty verbena, dahlias, eccremocarpus, philospermum, cobea, heliotrope etc.etc. and autumn cyclamens etc. I stayed out of doors for a large part of the day, and in the evening I read the memoirs of Lavalette. My nights were bad; I was often obliged to wake the maid, who was sleeping near me, when I had these attacks, a sort of spasm, which alarmed me extremely and left me breathless. I had only a faint hope of recovery, and my eyes filled with tears at the sight of the church seeing as my dwelling place all too soon the little graveyard of which it is the centre.

13 September 1831. Finally all the family arrived and I embraced them all with rapture. Afterwards I was almost prostrated by the extreme emotion which I felt on seeing them. Poor Horatia also wept very much on seeing me again. I did not find them changed or fatigued by their season in London, as I had expected. On the contrary, Caroline was very well, fresh, and prettier than I had ever seen her. Horatia also looked very well, but she was thin. Milady always very well. Mr F. a little changed. Since their arrival I have never for a moment ceased to feel how lucky I am, to be living peacefully with people whom I love so much, and who all day long give me proof of their friendship and care for me. There is no care lacking for my health. I see the doctor every day, I rise late, breakfast late, walk outside a little if the weather is fine, I have ridden on horseback several times; I don't like their riding horses here. My life passes so quietly, compared with what it has been, that if only I enjoyed good health, there is nothing more I could want for the present.

‌ *Thursday 22 September.* A few days after their arrival, Lady Ilchester came from Bowood with her granddaughter, Lady Theresa Strangways, to spend a day here. She is an excellent person and I was well pleased to see her again, also Lady Theresa, whom I had hardly seen since she was a small child. She is now a charming young person of 18 years, with an air that could not be more distinguished, the figure of a sylph, with great simplicity and an air of innocence and modesty without any gaucherie. At the same time came the Miss Gents and their mother. These young people are much sought after in society for their beautiful voices and their excellent manner of singing. They are certainly the most distinguished amateurs in this country. The elder, Maria, has a beautiful soprano voice, the younger, Honoria, has a most remarkable contralto. There is more feeling in her voice than in her sister's, although her execution is sometimes a little careless. But her voice is admirable. She sang in a manner which moved me deeply that lovely air *Se il mio nome saper voi bramate* [If you desire to know my name] (from Rossini's 'Barber') with such depth of passion and with such energy that nothing she sang afterwards could please me. The Miss Gents came on the 23rd of September. The weather has been continually splendid.

‌ *Monday 26 September.* Mrs Napier came with her children to visit us in the morning. Mr Moore came to dinner. He is gloomy. The Gents sang all the evening and the poet seemed charmed with their voices. Lord Kerry dined here yesterday; he is very tall but not improved in looks. He left us this morning.

‌ *Tuesday 27 September.* Mr Moore went away this morning, before breakfast, in the most treacherous manner. We sang nearly all *Tancredi* in the evening. Caroline sketched in the back yard.

‌ *2 October.* We played two charades last week. One was Cleopatra: Clef of Bluebeard; eau, Alexander pouring on to the sand the water which had been brought to him in a helmet in the desert of Gedrosie; and the whole, the death of Cleopatra. The other charade was Penelope: Pen, a scene from the *Barber of Seville*; Elope the abduction of Helen by Paris; and the whole Penelope recognising Ulysses while he bent his bow, for which the Miss Gents played and sang a very pretty cantata by Paer on the subject. Another day we played *Pacha Pas*; Caroline and Miss Maria Gent danced the gavotte, the cat changed into a woman for the second, and for the whole, a scene of a Pascha smoking in the midst of his wives.

‌ *Friday 7 October.* Mr and Mrs Bowles dined and slept. He was delighted with Caroline's Agnus Dei and her Gloria, her own composition.

‌ *Saturday 8 October.* Heard by express of the defeat of the Reform Bill in the House of Lords. Majority 41, 158-199. Mr and Mrs Bowles went away, the former very dejected.

‌ *Sunday 9th.* Read Lord Brougham's admirable speech.

‌ *Monday 10th.* I read aloud Bedreddin-Ali from the *Arabian Nights*.

‌ *Tuesday 11.* Mr John Strangways came from Abbotsbury.

‌ *Wednesday 12 October.* Lord Kerry and Mr Twopenny came: acted a charade, Passage. For Pas, the gavotte; the seven sages of Greece and the gold tripod; and the *Passage of the Red Sea*; we sang in chorus Rossini's *Prayer of Moses* amidst great applause.

Thursday 13 October. Picked Caroline's Indian Corn with the Miss Gents. Heard of Nottingham Castle being burnt!

Sunday 16. Wrote a letter to Mrs Hopwood, thanking her for the excellent letter I had received from her, in which she approves my plans and sees the need for a change of life and of air. I wrote that I did not feel well enough to dream of returning to her from here for at least two or three months; that it is necessary for me to go to Paris. In consequence I did not think that to return to her presently for a short stay would be of any use. She answered me in a very satisfactory manner, against my expectations, with a concern for my views and interests, for which I am most grateful, which I expressed as well as I could. Since I left them I have often had letters from Mary and from Miss Hopwood, who is now recovered. As for Mary, I regret her very much, as it seems very much that I shall not return to Hopwood, at least not very soon; also I am completely detached from that family, though with very bad health which does not improve. I am only a little better, but with all the same symptoms which I brought with me from Lancashire. Brilliant Italian sunset. Riots at Salisbury.

Monday 17 October. The Miss Gents returned from Bath, where they had been for two days. Mr Twopenny made some beautiful sketches of the Abbey. He is a lawyer with a great taste and a talent for architectural drawing. Mr Vivian and Mr Scrope came yesterday.

Tuesday 18 October. Lord Valletort came yesterday and sang in the evening with the Miss Gents.

Wednesday 19. Caroline rode with Lord V. Music in the evening.

Thursday 20. The Count Dietrichstein came. He is the son of the Governor of the Duke of Reichstadt, and attached to the Austrian Embassy. He is quite pleasant and talks of the King of Rome with great affection.

Friday 21. Count Danneskiold came to enlarge our party. He is a gay, lively little Dane and quite amusing in the country. Mr Vivian came to dinner. He lives 12 miles from Bath, at Claverton.

Saturday 22 October. Lord Valletort left.

Sunday 23. A day of great excitement. Caroline came into my room to show me a letter she had just received. With her simplicity and her natural modesty she found herself astounded at the choice, and much flattered. Lord Valletort was asking her hand in marriage. We were quite beside ourselves.

Monday 24. Mr Vivian went away. We have had a quantity of music all these days.

Tuesday 25 October. The two Miss Gents and their comic mother left for Leicestershire. They have been here nearly six weeks. Count Dietrichstein left to go shooting with Mr Vivian. Tampon has written a reply which she thinks is affirmative, but which is in fact a little ambiguous, not to say nonsensical.

Wednesday 26. Count Danneskiold left. He danced the mazurka yesterday evening.

Thursday. We were glad to be rid of all our guests. We were too preoccupied to enjoy their company.

Friday 28. They all went to Bowood. I was too ill to accept Lady Lansdowne's kind invitation.

Saturday 29. Caroline received a letter while at Bowood, which said that one could not understand her intentions as they were not clearly expressed. She answered in a much more explicit manner and in the affirmative.

Sunday 30 October. They all returned from Bowood.

Monday 31. Walked with Caroline and Horatia to the Hinders. I gave a complete suit of clothes to Jacob Hinder.

Monday 7 November. Received a letter from my brother Ferdinand from Santiago in Chile, which he has never left. The letter was written on 24th February 1831.

Tuesday November 5. Lord V. came this evening from Mount Edgcumbe, We were most moved, as if his visit concerned each one of us personally, since he came to take our treasure from us. Caroline has accepted him. Everyone agreed about his goodness, the integrity of his principles, his excellent heart and his sincerity. He is 24 years old and is generally considered a good-looking man. He is tall, with black hair and lively and expressive blue eyes and has a great air of masculinity.

Thursday 9. They went on horseback to Bowood to lunch.

Friday 11 November. Mr Moore dined and slept with us. He sang all the evening.

Saturday 12. Lord Lansdowne came for luncheon. One of these days I had a letter from Apollodore, from Calcutta, telling me that his wife and his little girl embarked on 1st May last on the *Lord Melville*, an English ship making for London. Mr Moore went away.

Sunday 13. They all went to dinner at Bowood. I was too ill to go.

Monday 14. Mr F. and Lord Valletort left for London this morning for business affairs. We have had Mr F.'s solicitor here and Lord Valletort's to make the marriage settlement. [...]

Tuesday 15 November. Lady Lansdowne and her daughter came.

Wednesday 16 November. Great dinner given by Lord Lansdowne in Devizes.

Thursday 17. Caroline and Milady left for London to buy her trousseau. Received a letter from Miss Hopwood with a present. She seems to miss me and is always interested in me. Went to Bowood with Horatia and Mr Talbot to dine and spend the night.

Tuesday 22. Caroline writes to ask me to be one of her bridesmaids, and I have promised that I will. On the day of their departure I went to dinner at Bowood with Horatia and Mr Talbot. There was only the family there; ourselves, Mr Moore and Mr Corry. Mr Moore sang all the evening. Lord Lansdowne seemed preoccupied and worried. We returned the next day. It has frozen hard for the last three days.

Thursday 24. Mr F. returned from London.

Friday 25. Long walk with Horatia and Mr F. to Ray-Mill.

Saturday 26 November. Milady and Caroline returned from London.

Monday 28. Lady Lansdowne came with Lord Henry and Lady Louisa.

Tuesday 29. Lord Valletort came at half past eleven. Terrible insurrection in Lyons. The workers have turned out their rulers and have taken possession of the town; they are 60,000 well-armed men. The Duke of Orleans and Marshal Soult have gone to restore order there. The carnage was terrible; it is said that 1600 men have perished.

Lord Ernest
Augustus
Valletort,
who proposed
to Caroline
Feilding on 23
October 1831

● *Wednesday 30.* I have written to Dr Kerrison in London to consult him and he has replied in detail to Mr Spencer about my state of health. I started to follow his treatment on Wednesday 23rd.

● *Thursday 1 December.* Caroline gave me her watch, which is a very pretty one, enamelled in blue and gold. Lord Lansdowne and Lady Louisa Fitzmaurice came, the former in very good spirits. He said that the Lyons affair is far from being over. The Emperor of Austria has just set free the unfortunate prisoners from Spielberg. He has also given asylum in Austria to the persecuted Poles. Caroline has received from her aunt Miss Feilding a very beautiful head-dress: it is a fine pearl, fairly large and of a most unusual egg-shape, suspended in the middle of a circle of most magnificent diamonds. From Lord Valletort she has gold chains and a seal etc. etc, and Horatia from the same some ear-rings, some little combs, a gold cross and chain, and some turquoises mounted in the form of an ear of corn and extremely pretty. Milady gave me a very beautiful comb, in tortoiseshell, which is modern, fashionable and very high. Mr F. has promised me a blue satin gown for the wedding. They are to be married in the chapel at Bowood. We are all very sad at Caroline's approaching departure, and at the same time happy to know she is in such good hands. Lord V. is *inamorato come un matto* [madly in love].

● *Friday 2.* Dull, dreary weather, but mild. Lord Henry Fitzmaurice came to lunch. He has returned from a tour in France and is always very polite. Mr Montgomerie arrived at dinner-time, he has come for the wedding. The cholera is making little progress in Sunderland. Unfortunately it has just broken out in Newcastle. Music in the evening *al solito* [as usual].

The troubles in Lyons seem to be calming down, but this calm is like a volcano, since the town is still in the hands of the workers. It has been surrounded by troops, but the people have declared that they will set fire to the town should a single soldier enter it. However, they say they are still faithful and obedient subjects of Louis Philippe.

● *Saturday 3 December.* A great disappointment. Lord Ilchester and his daughter Lady Theresa cannot come to the wedding because of the death of their brother-in-law and uncle Mr Henry Murray. We must search everywhere to find a replacement for that pretty bridesmaid. Lady Harriet Frampton and her daughter Louisa have been invited, but it is doubtful whether she would wish to undertake so long a journey to stay for so few days. We examined Caroline's trousseau. She has many beautiful dresses, veils, shawls etc. Rather a dreary evening. Caroline has a bad cold.

● *Sunday 4 December.* We have had the same weather for a whole week, dark, misty and mild. Milady is extremely low-spirited at her approaching loss and can hardly bear the idea of it; she suffers from too much agitation and is very much changed during this last fortnight. Today she has gone to Bowood to pour out her grief to her sister. She heard Mr Bowles, who preached an excellent sermon in the chapel. Caroline and Lord V. read their prayers together in Mr Talbot's study. She has received more presents from all her Talbot cousins, from Lord V. and from Miss

Mildmay; and Horatia has received a very pretty head-dress from her aunt, Miss Feilding. Horatia and Mr F. and Mr Montgomerie went to church.

I am now scribbling in this journal in despair of being able to sleep. It is 4 am. [...] Wrote a long letter to Mary Hopwood; I owed her one for a long time. I gave her details of the ceremony the day after tomorrow and asked her to send the two trunks which I left there. Played duets on the harp this evening with Horatia. The *Donna del Lago* seemed ravishing to me after all the mediocre music with which we are bored nowadays.

The three terrible men who traded in human flesh have been condemned to death. But the extraordinary thing is that Williams has made a confession after his death sentence, and it appears that it is not the little Italian who showed white mice in the London streets whom they have Burked (that is a new expression which means the most atrocious of all crimes, and it is reserved for this degraded century to see its birth.) To Burke, that is to say to take an individual by surprise, to kill him and to sell his body to the surgeons for dissection. Burke is the name of the monster who first committed this crime in Edinburgh two or three years ago – the prejudice in this country being so absurd that they do not give the bodies of unknown people who die in the hospitals for dissection, as is done in other countries. The art recedes for lack of means of studying anatomy and that is why the surgeons of this country are so much inferior to those in France. Therefore they pay very high prices for subjects and are not very scrupulous, it appears, about the manner in which those who sell them have procured them. A body generally costs 12 guineas; with the result that poverty has driven several villains to kill people for the reward they will gain. They generally start by being what are called resurrectionists. That is to say, they steal bodies from the graveyards by night – but they then discover that it is easier to take living people from the streets. Moreover, the bodies they acquire in this manner, being fresher, are worth more. The little boy whom one of them confesses to having killed in this way was an unfortunate little thing of 14 who was taking the cows to Smithfield Market. But the clothes which have been found buried in Bishop's garden: one of the murderers, prove that they have been doing this regularly for some time and that several women and children who have suddenly disappeared have been killed in this manner. Truly I believe that this country is a hot-bed of crime and immorality and the newspapers and modern works are beginning to admit this.

This morning I tried on my white satin dress. It is very pretty and well made, but I fear I shall not have the opportunity to wear it the day after tomorrow. If Miss Louisa Frampton does not come to make an even number of four I shall not be able to be a bridesmaid, the custom here being always to have an even number. Horatia and Lady Louisa Fitzmaurice are the first pair; Lady Theresa Strangways and I were to have been the second. It has been decided that we should all go to dinner at Bowood the day after tomorrow and they will be married after dinner at 9 o'clock in the evening, in the chapel. We shall return afterwards to have tea here, and we shall leave the young couple in possession of that beautiful dwelling house.

Lady Lansdowne and her children will return with us for two days, to leave them together.

I wish I could lie down and sleep, but I no longer dare try to do so. I am beginning to feel hungry and am horribly tired.

I have read the *Memoirs* of Count Lavalette, which are very interesting: *The Loves of the Poets* by Mrs Jameson, which is rather an insipid work, especially the second volume: the charming letters of Mme de Villars for the third or fourth time, always with renewed pleasure and the *Life of Lord Byron* by Thomas Moore. His letters and papers could not be more amusing, but I don't in the least like the few reflections which Mr Moore has inserted, there is nothing new, nothing frank, it seems to be the work of a Jesuit, and although he says he has written this book to vindicate his memory, as a friend, it seems that he has done it more harm than a declared enemy would have done. I am in the middle of the second volume. I read also the memoirs of Constant, *valet de chambre* of the Emperor Napoleon; they were nothing but rhapsodies and repetitions of what everyone has read a hundred times.

Monday 5 December. Mr King, Mr F.'s lawyer, came this morning to settle those deeds, which everyone has signed, including Caroline, who is cast down and indisposed. How much better they do these things in France; here it is just like preparing for death; which has often made me wish not to have been present. Lord Mount Edgcumbe (father of Lord V.) came to lunch with his inseparable companion, his dog Pepper, who is very ugly but sweet-tempered and intelligent, and he enlivened the languishing conversation. However, Lord V. is very gay, very animated and talks agreeably on all sorts of subjects. He normally lives in his beautiful estate of Mount Edgcumbe in Devonshire, near to Plymouth, which everyone says is one of the most picturesque places in the country, situated on a hill bathed by the waters of the sea. Lord M. is 67 years old and in physique seems older than his years; he is lame, having broken his leg some years ago. But apart from that his wit and his manners are young. Caroline did not dine with us. In the evening we played a little music, but it is difficult to please Lord M., who, although a very distinguished lover of music, detests modern music, Rossini, his imitators, (these last with justification) and even Handel, the god of harmony in England.

Neither Lady Henrietta Frampton nor her daughter have arrived, so I shall not be a bridesmaid. We also waited in vain for Sir Charles Lemon – so it will not be a very gay wedding. This evening Mr Talbot lit Bengal candles in the cloisters, which produced a charming effect and picked out the gothic arches surrounded by creepers, showing to advantage the beauties of their architecture.

Tuesday 6 December 1831. Caroline's wedding day. The brilliant sun when I got up was a good omen. The bells and peals in the village were ringing gaily to celebrate this day. I quickly went to embrace the dear child who was still in bed. I lay near her and we chatted peacefully for half an hour. The morning passed very quickly and after lunch we left for Bowood; many villagers and poor people lined the road right up to the top of Bowden Hill. Mr Talbot had caused bread to be given to each of 1400 poor people who made the air ring with acclamations along our way and with cheers and Talbot for ever!! This moved us to tears. On arrival at Bowood, Caroline shut herself in her room and did not dine with us. Lord Mount Edgcumbe enlivened the meal a little. Afterwards we went to the bride's room to help her to dress; she looked charming, a thousand times more interesting than I have ever seen her, and quite calm, but suffering from a cold. She had a white satin gown and over that one of lace [...]; on her forehead the beautiful Ferronière composed of a superb pearl surrounded by diamonds, which her Aunt Matilda had given her; a pretty garland of orange blossom, my wedding present, placed right on her forehead and intermingled with her hair; a very beautiful veil of Brussels lace, and no other jewels. She was as beautiful as an angel, with her usual calm and simplicity increased by an air of natural modesty which made her irresistible. She went down to the drawing room conducted by her father, who was making great efforts to control his emotion. When we entered the chapel, the organ played, a cloud of incense spread around us and the ceremony began. Mr Paley read the prayers in a moving and resonant voice, and married them; he looked like a saint while he joined their hands and received their promises; he partook of the general emotion. Milady was dissolved in tears the whole time; no-one was calm at that moment. Caroline replied to the priest's questions in quite a confident voice; she was pale but composed. Afterwards we all signed the deed of marriage and returned to the drawing room, where Caroline threw herself into her father's arms and gave vent to her tears. I embraced her several times in a state of mind difficult to describe. Lord Valletort seemed quite beside himself; he shook me by the hand several times in a convulsive agitation. At last we had to leave her. She asked me to have a word with her in private and gave me a sealed paper which she asked me not to open until I went to bed.

We left them together in the drawing room and returned to Lacock with Lady Lansdowne and her children. Before dinner the young Lord Henry Fitzmaurice lit several fireworks on the terrace for us. The two bridesmaids were Horatia and Lady Louisa Fitzmaurice. Lord Mount Edgcumbe left for London after the ceremony, and after having kissed Caroline very tenderly two or three times, calling her his daughter, his dear daughter.

On returning to Lacock I opened the paper and found a deed of gift for my life, which Lord Valletort had given me by request of his wife. I was stupefied with astonishment and with gratitude and wished I could have expressed it straight away to the one who has been so good to me. I went to bed quite distracted.

Wednesday 7 December. I wrote to Lady Valletort to thank her and to express to her my profound gratitude and my affection for her although she already knew it well. Wrote to Miss Feilding to give her a description of yesterday's ceremony. A line came from Lord Valletort; they will not leave Bowood tomorrow, but the day after tomorrow, and they are well. Everyone has written to C. Poor Horatia is sad; quite naturally, it is a great loss to her. Lord Henry Fitzmaurice gave us a little firework display in the cloister. Prepared some tapestry work for Horatia. We were all sad and idle.

 Thursday 8 December. Gloomy weather, mild but rainy. Wrote to Maman to tell her about the wedding and about the unexpected present which I owe to C.! She will be very happy about it. [...] I read the *Life of Lord Byron* for two hours. Milady and Lady Lansdowne went out in the carriage; Lady Louisa, Lord Henry, Mr Montgomerie and Mr F. on horseback; Horatia and myself on foot. We walked in the cloisters to take exercise, as we couldn't put a foot out of doors because of the torrential rain. We weighed ourselves; I weigh 109 lbs or 7 stone 11 pounds and Horatia 108 lbs; Mr F. 13 stone. In the evening read several amusing passages from Lady E.'s album, a racy description of the apartment of Lady Elisabeth Forster (the 2nd Duchess of Devonshire) by Mr Hare.

 Friday 9 December. Pouring rain all morning. Lady Lansdowne returned to Bowood at 12 o'clock, where we joined her at 4. Quiet evening. Looked over many books. Read a little of *Delphine* of Mme de Staël. Lord and Lady Valletort set off this morning from this place at 12 for Redlynch. She wrote last night to her father and mother: they say here that she was not well: Lady L. missed her on purpose by a quarter of an hour only. Beautiful house and comfortable to perfection! [...]

 Saturday 10 December. Fine and mild weather. I was harassed with my wretched night. Breakfasted in my room. Walked in the shrubbery with Mr F., Horatia and Mr Montgomerie. Milady and Lady Lansdowne went to Compton Basset to visit Mrs Heneage. I did not dine with them. The Duke of Orleans and Marshal Soult have entered Lyons with troops and have been well received. However it does not appear that the authorities are yet recognised.

 Sunday 11. As on the previous night there was terrible wind and rain. Read *Delphine* for several hours during my interrupted slumbers of the early morning. Saw plaster models (quite small) of the marbles from the Parthenon. What majesty, strength, spirit, grace and beauty there are in these marble figures. They have more life in them than living people of today. Mr and Mrs Moore and their small son Russell came to church, as well as Mrs and Mr Bowles. The latter preached an extempore sermon. He has a most moving voice and an impressive eloquence. He took his text from Isaiah Chapter 52. His poetic language is so different from what one usually hears! They left after the service. They suggested that I should visit Bath with them on Tuesday to hear Paganini, but that could not be arranged. Mr Moore was very gay and very talkative. He sang charming songs all the evening; I am very fond of his Irish melodies. I dined with them in spite of feeling unwell, not wishing to miss the poet's agreeable conversation. It is so seldom that one meets people of a natural and cultivated wit who are prepared to use it for the enjoyment of others; moreover he expresses himself in such an easy manner, without a touch of pedantry or affectation, that in listening to him one is conscious only of pleasure in his superiority, without being in the least overcome by it. He is essentially a man of the world of the greatest wit, and one forgets the writer – speaking of a lady yesterday at dinner he said 'She is exceedingly pleasant, good and sensible, although a poet', which made us all laugh.

 Monday 12. Horatia has received a letter from Lady Valletort from Redlynch, full of memories of her childhood which that place recalls to her. We tried with Mr Moore some of Haydn's sacred music, but I no longer have any voice. Lady Lansdowne showed us a superb present she had received from India, from Lady William Bentinck. It is real cashmere all embroidered with gold from Delhi, one of the most beautiful I have ever seen. There was also a fan from India, all in gold and silver and worked in a marvellous pattern in imitation of lace. Mr Moore said it gave the idea of the magnificence of the East even more that the cashmere. We returned at 1 o'clock. It was shocking weather; the river has run over all our fields. There was thunder and lightning and a wind which seemed to threaten to engulf us under the ruins of the old abbey. We were expecting Mr and Mrs Seymour and their two daughters from Dorset, but no doubt the bad weather has alarmed them.We are threatened with being completely submerged; we seem to be in the middle of a huge lake.

Tuesday 13. Today it is a week since Caroline's wedding. Mr Talbot had a letter from her this morning from Melbury. It was fine this morning and the sun shone on the waters, but the sky looks as if it will discharge a lot more. The Seymours arrived at 4 o'clock, Mrs S. has the remains of a beauty which must have been ravishing. She is the sister of the Lord Rivers who was drowned last year and the aunt of the present one. She spent several years in Italy in her youth and returned with her daughters two or three years ago: she is said to paint very well: however she is rather silent, not very animated and her conversation does not fulfil the promise of her appearance and her manner. The father is very lively, witty and a great lover of the fine arts. The two girls are very pretty, the elder tall, dark and well made, with a carriage of the head which reminds me of Eliza Hunlocke; the younger, called Grace, is small and with little or no figure, but her face is charming, her complexion of a radiant whiteness and very fine, and there is much delicacy in her features. She seems to have more spirit than the others. They paint and are musical, but they have lost their voices, and they never perform in front of their father, who is a merciless critic. Horatia and I played many duets for four hands on the piano in the evening. Dinner was rather dull.

Wednesday 14. [...] Everyone has gone to Bowood to show the house to the Seymours who are great friends of Lady Henrietta Frampton. I stayed here with Horatia and helped her to put new strings on the harp. Then we went for a walk but the rain chased us into the cloisters which are well suited for taking exercise. Prepared the wools for the tapestry which I am going to begin. Played duets for harp and piano with Horatia and several tunes from operas from memory. Went to my room at midnight. This morning I had a letter from Mary Hopwood; she spent a fortnight at Croxteth with Lord Sefton where she enjoyed herself very much, also at Norton with Sir Richard Brook where there were 23 people. Miss Hopwood is a little better; now they have all returned to Hopwood.

Thursday 15. [...] My mother says that she has now decided to see the little society of the country. Each in turn gives a soirée in Brunoy where they play at Boston and at écarté. This is a relaxation, it is not very amusing but it is better than nothing. She also will give a party. She is pressing me to come and join her. I wrote again to Miss Feilding, who wished it.

It has been gloomy weather and wet, and we have not been able to go out. Played at battledore and shuttlecock and *aux grâces* in the Hall with the two Miss Seymours, Mr Montgomerie, Mr Talbot and Horatia: these two gentlemen seem to admire the beauty of these ladies greatly. I do not feel much attracted to them, although they are good, sweet and very polite. They have no conversation, and are lifeless and languid. Time passes very heavily in their company. Mr Vivian was added to our company for dinner, to give the ladies one more admirer. Mr Moore came too. He was not very gay at dinner, but he sang all the evening, very well and with a very lively air. [...] 3 o'clock in the morning, scribbling in this miserable journal.

Friday 16 December. [...] Betty Vickery looked after me from 2 o'clock until midnight. [...]

Saturday 17. Mr and Mrs Seymour and their daughters left as well as Mr Vivian. There was a rainstorm again yesterday and the river has flooded. But it is fine again this morning. I had a friendly letter from Caroline. She is at Abbotsbury, very happy, she says, but not forgetting any of her friends, nor the happiness of past days. They go to Melbury to see Lord Ilchester next Monday. Lord Valletort is full of tenderness and of attentive care for her.

Mrs Nicholl, who is now at Bowood, came with two Miss Selwyns and Lady Louisa Fitzmaurice for luncheon. Mr Vivian went to see the pictures at Bowood with Mr F. and returned home after. I tried to sing a little in the evening and played with Horatia on the pianoforte. Rainy weather. Another flood and hurricane.

Sunday 18 December. Fine morning with very cold wind. [...] Read the first volume of *Amelia* by Fielding. [...] Walked with Horatia and Morphine on the road. [...] Read several of Milady's extracts books. Copied some verses of Bowles' etc. etc. Very cold night. [...]

Monday 19 December. [...] Mr F. and Milady went to Bath to see Lady Mary Cole; she is there to drink the waters. Cold day, foggy. I did not go out. Played on the harp with H. in the evening. Read the *Life of Lord Byron* and *Amelia*.

Tuesday 20. Received a very kind and agreeable letter from Mrs Starky from Bowness. She had been ill with an attack of something like Miss Hopwood. The cholera has reached Hull and is spreading.

Wednesday 21 December. [...] Beautiful sunny day. Walked two hours in the garden with Horatia. Played with her several duets in the evening. Practised a little on the pianoforte. Wrote a letter to Lady Valletort at Melbury. Begun yesterday my tapestry work, two beautiful Chinese pheasants. Mr Montgomerie and Mr Feilding went shooting all the morning.

Thursday 22. Walked in the village with Horatia. Worked at my tapestry. Began a letter to Mary. Saw with great joy in the paper the arrival at St Helena of the ship *Lord Melville* from Bengal. I hope not to be disappointed, and that it may bring my poor sister safely. I read the account of the law suit for the will of the Duke

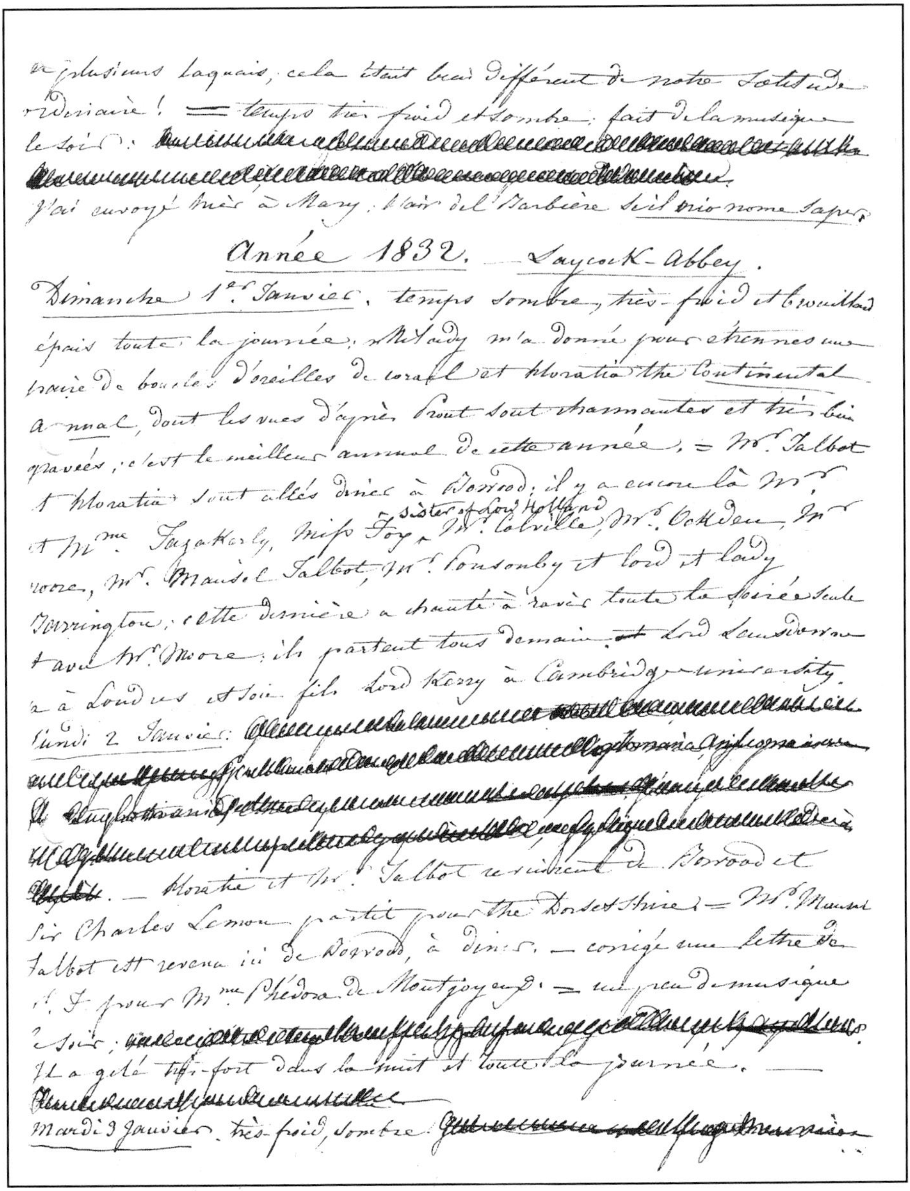
de plusieurs laquais; cela était bien différent de notre solitude
ordinaire! = temps très froid et sombre: fait de la musique
le soir: [illegible]
[illegible]
J'ai envoyé hier à Mary: l'air del Barbiere Se il mio nome saper.

Année 1832. — Laycock-Abbey.

Dimanche 1er Janvier. temps sombre, très froid et brouillard
épais toute la journée: Milady m'a donné pour étrennes une
paire de boucles d'oreilles de corail et Horatia the Continental
annual, dont les vues d'après Prout sont charmantes et très bien
gravées; c'est le meilleur annual de cette année. = Mr. Talbot
et Horatia sont allés dîner à Bowood; il y a encore là Mr.
et Mme Fazakerly, Miss Fox (sister of Lord Holland) Mr. Colville, Mr. Ottley, Mr
Moore, Mr. Mansel Talbot, Mr. Ponsonby et Lord et Lady
Torrington; cette dernière a chanté à ravir toute la soirée seule
et avec Mr. Moore; ils partent tous demain, et Lord Lansdowne
va à Londres et son fils Lord Kerry à Cambridge university.
Lundi 2 Janvier: [illegible]
[illegible]
— Horatia et Mr. Talbot reviennent de Bowood et
Sir Charles Lemon partit pour the Dorsetshire. = Mr. Mansel
Talbot est revenu ici de Bowood, à dîner. — corrigé une lettre de
M. F. pour Mme Phédora de Montjoye. — un peu de musique
le soir; [illegible]
Il a gelé très fort dans la nuit et toute la journée. —
[illegible]
Mardi 3 Janvier. très froid, sombre. [illegible]

A page from Amélina's journals, written in 1832. When she re-read the journals in 1870, the mature Amélina corrected names and often deleted whole paragraphs of Bourbon against Mme la Baronne de Feuchères. Much guile is being used to make the king appear in an unfavourable light. The proceedings against Mme de Feuchère have been instituted by the Princes of Rohan. M. Hennequin, their lawyer, is a violent Carlist.

Friday 23. [...] Walked to Ray-Bridge with Horatia and Mr F., who went to pay a visit to the Miss Awdrys at their cottage. I walked about alone while waiting for them, and made Morphine take a swim. [...] The weather was magnificent – cloudless and not too cold. Played on the harp and piano in the evening.

Saturday 24 December. It was very fine weather and I walked for 2 hours on Bowden Hill with Horatia. We visited all the poor people on the hill to find out what they would most need when the money is distributed from the savings they have taken to the club each week throughout the year, and to which a third has been added, to pay for winter clothes, fuel, blankets etc. etc. We were very alarmed by the appearance of three sailors of a terrifying aspect who demanded alms of us in an insolent manner on the road and who seemed to be lying in wait for us. We sent them to the Abbey to get rid of them, but this was not easy to do. At length our terror made us ask a labourer from the farm of Beaulieu Court Priory to accompany us to the house. Sir Charles Lemon and Lady Louisa Fitzmaurice came to lunch. Music and a little singing in the evening with Mr Montgomerie.

Sunday 25. Christmas Day. Beautiful weather. Went to church with Mr F., Horatia and Mr M. Milady went to church at Bowood. Lord Lansdowne has arrived. Walked with H., Mr M. and Mr F. along the canal. In Caroline's name Horatia distributed 3 lb. of bacon to each of 12 poor women who had been previously chosen. In a poor parish like this, that is a rich present.

Monday 26. Fine weather. A little frosty. Lady Lansdowne, Miss Fox (Lord Holland's sister), Lady Louisa Fitzmaurice, Lord Henry Fitzmaurice, and Mr Guthrie came to lunch. [...] also wrote to Mary Hopwood to ask if her mother would recommend Mr Talbot's courier, Giovanni Perey, to Mr Bold Houghton, who wishes to take him into his service. We had a large dinner party of rural neighbours. Mr and Mrs Locke and two of their daughters, Mr Moore the poet, (so rural!) his wife and his two young sons, Mr and Mrs Joy, whom he has recently married. She is very young and pretty and very affected, but far from the flowery portrait which he had painted of her. Mr Christopher Talbot has come to stay for several days. I excused myself from the dinner which, I am told, was rather boring. The elder Miss Locke is a great wit, a poet and a satirist. She is amusing, but not at all pretty. Her sister sings very badly, with one of the best voices one could have – but her mouth shuts firmly without method etc. etc. We played a little music.

1832 *Sunday 1 January.* Gloomy weather. Very cold and a thick fog the whole day. Milady gave me two coral ear-rings as a New Year gift and Horatia the *Continental Annual* whose views after Prout are charming and very well engraved; it is the best annual of this year. Mr Talbot and Horatia went to dine at Bowood; also there still are Mr and Mrs Fazakerly, Miss Fox, sister of Lord Holland, Mr Colville, Mr Ockden, Mr Moore, Mr Mansel Talbot, Mr Ponsonby and Lord and Lady

Amélina with Caroline (seated) and Horatia, whose musical education she guided from their childhood.

Barrington; the latter sang divinely all the evening, alone and with Mr Moore. They all leave tomorrow, Lord Lansdowne goes to London and his son Lord Kerry to Cambridge University.

Monday 2 January. Horatia and Mr Talbot returned from Bowood and Sir Charles Lemon left for Dorsetshire. Mr Mansel Talbot returned here from Bowood for dinner. Corrected a letter for Mr F. for Mrs Phedora de Montjoyeux. Some music in the evening. It froze very hard during the night and all the day.

Tuesday 3 January. Very cold, gloomy. Went to Chippenham with Milady after luncheon. Shopped in the shops owned by Mr Talbot's supporters. [...] A little music in the evening. Caroline writes that she will come soon, this week.

Wednesday 4 January. The same gloomy cold weather. A sky which threatens a snowfall. The news in the papers is rather disquieting. They speak of a war caused by the stupid king of Holland and by the insatiable ambition of that Cossack Nicholas!

Thursday 5. Excessively cold. Frost and fog. I walked with Horatia, Mr Montgomerie and Mr Feilding on Bowden Hill and in the village. Yesterday we walked with Mr Mansel Talbot poor man he is so changed! if the cause of his melancholy is really the one people believe, I would never have believed it! On the other hand he does not deserve too much of our compassion since it is his fault. [...]

Friday 6. Received a very friendly letter from Miss Matilda Feilding in answer to two of mine on the subject of Caroline's marriage. Mr F. also had a letter from her (from Lady Valletort) which announces that she and her husband will arrive this evening for dinner; which rather annoyed them, as Horatia and Mr F. are engaged to go to dinner and stay the night at Farley Castle with Mr Houlton. It is very cold and gloomy. Mr Mansel Talbot left at 5 for Bath; he goes from there to Melbury. Mr F. and Horatia left for Farley Castle. Lord and Lady Valletort arrived at 6.30. She seems very well, and has a gay and happy look, fresh as a rose, but however very little fatter. Milord has grown a moustache to please his wife; I think it is going to look well, but at present it seems that his features have taken on a wild appearance which I don't like. I was suffering all day from another [illegible] ceaselessly before my eyes with all its consequences. [...] Lady E. could not have been more concerned about it.

⁤ *Saturday 7 January.* Lord Henry Fitzmaurice came. Mr F. and Horatia returned from Farley Castle. [...]

⁤ *Sunday 8 January 1832.* Things are not going at all as I should like. There is one of us who appears disagreeable and obstinate. However the lady does not seem to notice it, for her, on the contrary, he is perfect. Doubtless politics are the cause, since there is talk of creating 40 peers to help the passage of the Reform Bill. We assure ourselves that his bad temper has no other cause.

⁤ *Monday 9.* Rain all the day. Lord V. has recovered his good temper. Mrs Houlton of Farley Castle came with her two elder daughters, Isabella and Elisa. Mr Moore came also. Dinner as boring as it could be, evening almost the same, apart from the guitar playing of Miss Isabella; she played marvellously and produced all sorts of charming effects in the Spanish manner. It is very seldom that one hears this instrument played in this manner. She sings also and has a pretty voice. Her sister has a contralto voice with a few good notes, but as for their beauty, it is not up to much. They are silent and not at all gay. Caroline looked charming, dressed in a beautiful gown of white cashmere which suits her wonderfully, her hair with a headband and a gold head-dress, long golden ear-rings, a heart and a large cross of the same on a black velvet ribbon, a boa of sable; but one needs to see her, a description gives scarcely any idea! They played duets, I played the harp a little, Mr Montgomerie, Lord Valletort and Mr Moore sang a little.

⁤ *Tuesday 10 January.* Breakfast for 12 people crowded round the table. Mr Moore went to Sloperton to write; he is returning for dinner. Music in the evening. Caroline charming in a gown of black velvet with gold jewels. Miss Isabella played divinely on her guitar which Mr F. had fetched from Farley Castle. Sang with Mr Moore and Lord V. Miss Elisa Houlton has great pretentions in music. She sang two psalms of her own composition.

⁤ *Wednesday 11.* Mrs Houlton and her daughters left, also Mr Moore. Lord and Lady Lansdowne came to dine, the former very gay, very friendly and chatty; which did not in the least cheer up Lord V., who gave vent to his bad temper towards a minister, who however was so good, so friendly, to him in particular. Music in the evening. Played on the harp and sang with Lord V., who is making some progress, thanks to his wife. She is always the same, that is to say, charming, pretty, sweet, good-tempered, without the shadow of affectation. This evening she was in a cherry-coloured gown of gros d'été which made her look ravishing.

Thursday 12. Lord and Lady Valletort, Mr Talbot, Horatia and Mr Feilding went to dine at Bowood. [...] At 3 a.m. I met Caroline in the gallery in her dressing gown, who was alarmed to see me so ill. I scolded her for not being yet in bed. She came to see me in my room and asked me how I liked her nightcap; Lord V. had put it on her! They are a couple of children together! They laugh and talk and never go to bed till 3 o'clock. I spoke to Caroline severely about this, after which she retired. I lay down and dismissed Lydia, but it was impossible to stay in bed. I choked with convulsions which became so strong that I woke Horatia who was most alarmed. I lay in her bed, where I could not stay, and got up again and walked all over the house until 6.30 in the morning, when I managed to sleep a disturbed sleep for two hours. And this is the kind of night I have been having for the past six months. It is not living, it is dying little by little.

Friday 13 January. However, I walked a lot, although it was very cold – but I find that fresh air does me good; I am always better out of doors. Miss Fox came to dinner, she is Lord Holland's sister, extremely friendly, clever and good. Caroline was preparing for her departure, and dressed her husband as a Turk with one of her costumes. It is one of her weaknesses, she delights in extraordinary costumes; he was very handsome, with a blue striped turban, smoking a long pipe, his legs crossed, sitting on a sofa. (I had a very good night.)

Saturday 14. Wrote to Mrs Starkey at Bowness and to Mary Hopwood. Walked a little. Lord and Lady Valletort left this morning for Twickenham to stay with Lord Mount Edgcumbe, where they will stay only until tomorrow, Tuesday, when they go to London for the opening of Parliament. Their London house is Queen Street, Mayfair, No. 18, but it is only a pied à terre. They both appeared very happy.

Sunday 15 January. Very fine and cold. I walked with Horatia. Received at last a letter from Mary, franked by Lord Wilton. She is enjoying herself very much and has visited Hawarden Castle in Cheshire, the home of Sir Stephen Glynne; Lord and Lady Robert Grosvenor were there, and Mr Dick Wilbraham, who had tenderly demanded news of me. They have had plenty of company at Hopwood: among others Mr and Mrs Petre (who was the pretty Adela Howard from Corby Castle) etc. etc. Mr Charles Hall, son of the late Dean of Durham and nephew of Mrs Hopwood, is dead and has left his Bavarian widow and a quantity of children in poverty. Caroline wrote her mother a few words from Marlborough. She was obliged to warm herself by drinking hot water with sugar and brandy, which rather annoyed her father, who thought it not very elegant. Sang a little in the evening. Copied a Neapolitan air for Mr Montgomerie, *Fenesta vascia e padrona crudele* [Closed window! Ah cruel mistress].

Monday 16. Mr Montgomerie left at 7 a.m. He goes to Richmond, then to London and finally to Norfolk...I played on the harp a great deal, and I walked in the village. It was cold but not frosty.

Tuesday 17 January. Gloomy, cold without frost, damp, misty. Mr Talbot left this morning for a visit to Dorset to Mr Seymour, whose daughters are so pretty.

Caroline has written to her mother from Twickenham where she is staying with her father-in-law, Lord Mount Edgcumbe, who received her with great kindness and has made her a present of a bracelet in very good taste, made of very fine emeralds, and pearls.

∽ *Wednesday 18.* Walked to Wick Farm with Mr F. and Horatia. Played a great deal on the harp. Delightful weather.

∽ *Thursday 19.* Cold and foggy. Milady and Horatia went to dine at Bowood. I started to copy out Mr F.'s genealogy.

∽ *Friday 20.* I walked alone in the fields. Pleasant weather.

∽ *Saturday 21.* Walk on Bowden Hill with Horatia and Mr F. Met Lord Henry Fitzmaurice who came to tea with us with us. Cold damp weather.

∽ *Sunday 22.* Caroline's birthday; she is 24 today. Therefore I wrote to her. Took a walk. Mr Methuen's son came to dine and stay the night.

∽ *Monday 23.* Walked a lot. Fine weather. Played the harp.

∽ *Tuesday 24.* Received a very friendly letter from Caroline. Went to a ball in Chippenham. There were very few people there and it is was much less enjoyable. They say that many people came to the costume ball on Saturday, who did not wish to go to two balls in one week. Miss Sarah Locke is really very beautiful, but her elder sister is bold and has an appearance and manner which one does not normally meet in good company. They say she has much wit, but it is strangely abused! Mr Isaac Horlock is remarkably handsome; his brother William who 'keeps the hounds' is ill-bred, but the latter's wife is quite pretty and distinguished. The whole of Mr Neeld's faction (opposed to Mr Talbot) were there: his two sisters Mrs White and Mrs Boldero who could not be more common in their appearance, his brother is a little better. In fact there was no-one there of any interest, except Mrs Napier and her two elder daughters, who were there, also all the Starkys etc. etc.

∽ *Wednesday 25.* Had a long letter from Mary. They have been to Heaton and again have the house full of people. Took a walk. Mr Heneage and Mr Paul Methuen (the son) came to hunt and to dine afterwards. Mr Talbot arrived in the evening from Moreton. Tremendous rainstorm, in which we were caught.

∽ *Thursday 26.* Packed up the harp and began preparations for our departure. It froze in the night. What extraordinary weather! Lady Lansdowne, Lady Louisa and Mr Guthrie walked from Bowood and lunched with us. It is cold and damp. Mr Talbot set off this evening for London.

∽ *Friday 27 January.* Packed all day. I walked in the village. It freezes and thaws alternately. Very curious weather.

∽ *Saturday 28.* Did the Feilding's genealogy. We are very peaceful alone in the old abbey.

∽ *Sunday 29 January.* Walked a little. Went with Milady and Horatia to distribute the Sunday School prizes. Read the Bible with Horatia.

∽ *Monday 30 January 1832.* Preparations for departure. Did the F. genealogy.

∽ *Tuesday 31.* We all left Lacock at midday (in the Berline and the coupé.) Dined at

Speen-Hill, arrived in London at midnight. Cold weather, a little rain. Found Mr Talbot at the fireside.

Although the following extracts refer to events in London rather than Lacock, they are included here because they tell the story of an important chapter in the life of the Feilding family in which Amélina was closely involved. They also illustrate the very different, culturally rich life she led in London.

◍ *Wednesday 1 February.* Unpacked. The house has been newly painted. I have my old room, which had been altered for Horatia. It now has French windows. Horatia has Caroline's old room. Caroline came this morning and again this evening after dinner. She is very well.

◍ *Thursday 2 February.* Sir Charles Lemon came this morning. Milady and Horatia dined at Lord and Lady Valletort's with Lord M. I remained at home with Mr Talbot and Mr F. [...]

◍ *Friday 3 February.* I wrote a long letter to Mary Hopwood. Caroline came at 1 o'clock to ask Horatia to go to an opera rehearsal for *L'Esule di Roma* by Donizetti, which has its first performance tomorrow. It seems that the music and the singers are mediocre. [...]

◍ *Saturday 4.* I went out on foot with Mr F. and Horatia. We went to visit Lady Valletort whom we found at breakfast, looking so calm and happy, as if she had been married for 20 years. Milord appeared later; they both get up terribly late! Their house is extremely small, but big enough for the two of them. They have a large and very good Broadwood piano: two pretty little statues of Amorini, one by Thorwaldsen, the other by an Englishman, a bust of Lord V. made in Rome by Thorwaldsen, which is not a good likeness. We soon left them and the rain hastened our return. Caroline and Lord V. dined with us and we all went together to the Adelphi Theatre to see *Robert the Devil*, an imitation of Meyerbeer's opera, which is the rage in Paris at the moment. It is extraordinary the way they can produce such effects in such a small theatre. The decorations and scenery are excellent; especially a scene set in the church of the monastery of St. Rosaline near Palermo, showing the statues of the nuns reclining on their tombs and coming to life little by little at the voice of a spirit from the underworld. This produced an effect the like of which I have never seen in the theatre. Some of them descended slowly from their niches where they were placed along the aisles of the church, others raised themselves from the depth of the earth, others left their tombs and appeared to live. The faint rays of a hidden lamp fall on some of these figures so as to make them stand out and give them a deathly appearance. It made one shudder. Afterwards we had *The Lions of Mysore*. It is a critique of the play at Drury Lane in which lions, boas, tigers, hyenas, kangaroos etc. all appear. Here all the animals are represented by actors, and although nothing but a little farce it is quite amusing and I enjoyed it. It is not the same with the pantomime which is the dullest and most common of all those that I have seen, that is to say, *Harlequin, Little BoPeep*, or *The Old Woman who lived in a Shoe*! Nonsense, with no gaiety. We returned to take tea at the house at 11.30, but Caroline returned home, although at the bottom of her heart perhaps she would have been quite pleased to be of our party. Tomorrow she goes to Twickenham to spend the day and night with her father-in-law, Lord Mount Edgcumbe.

Sunday 5 February. I went to mass at the Bavarian chapel where they perform very well all the beautiful masses of Mozart, Beethoven, Haydn etc. etc. The choir is almost too numerous for the space. I heard a very good sermon there. [...] Mr Kit Talbot and Mr John Strangways dined at the house.

Monday 6. Lord Auckland and Mr John Strangways dined here. The former is very much changed. He seemed pleased to see me, which touched me extremely, because I was no less pleased to see him again. He is very much overwhelmed with affairs and with the cares of state. [...]

Tuesday 7 February. Received a letter from Mrs H. full of reproaches, although she makes out that she is not reproaching me. She accuses me of having sacrificed her daughter to my affection for the F. family, and is impatient because I have not yet left for France, where I might hope to be cured, so she says. But spite and jealousy are present in every line. What state am I in to undertake a long journey! Caroline came in for a moment before dinner. She had been visiting Lady Pembroke and Lady Sandwich.

A conspiracy has been discovered in Paris which had for its aim the assassination of the king and the royal family during a ball at the Tuileries, on the 2nd of last month. The conspirators had procured keys to the part of the Louvre which communicates with the château. They had false patrols in Paris at various points. But the police, warned in advance, had upset all their plans by cutting their various communications. There has been fighting in several places. One sergeant was killed, 60 men wounded and 250 prisoners taken by the police. It seems that people of all parties were involved: Carlists, Bonapartists, Republicans etc., so that one cannot imagine how all these miserable people had the same plan. [...]

Wednesday 8 February. I slept after all the agonies of the night from 4am. until 10. It was delightful weather, with plenty of sun. We walked in the park, Mr F., Horatia and myself. Sir Charles Lemon and Lady Lansdowne came. The Queen, who is very fond of Lord Valletort, sent him and Lady Valletort tickets for her box this evening at Covent Garden, and Caroline offered to take Horatia and me as well. They were giving *The Provoked Husband*, an old comedy by —. It is a chilly play and not very interesting, except for the last scene, which Charles Kemble and his daughter Fanny acted with plenty of feeling. The first part of the role of Lady Townley was very badly acted by Fanny, who gave the look and manners of a rope-dancer to a woman of quality who was mad for entertainment and wildly extravagant, but that does not give taste or manners. She spoiled it completely, except in the sentimental scene, in my opinion she is quite insupportable in this role. After this we had a Harlequin farce on the subject of Tom Thumb, which was very well acted by a little Miss Poole, who is no more than 11 or 12 years old. The scenery very nice and it is one of the most amusing farces I have seen. We all returned to take tea at home. Caroline and Lord V. did not leave until 1 am.

Thursday 9 February. Horrible weather, rain, black fog etc. Went out in the carriage with Horatia, Milady and Mr F. We went to the Soho Square Bazaar. Caroline and Lord Valletort dined here. A little music in the evening.

Friday 10. Walked with Mr F. and Horatia in St James's Park and Carlton Terrace, where there are the most superb new houses. Went to see Caroline, whom we found at breakfast. Met Lord Lansdowne in St. James's Park. Received a letter from Mary.

Saturday 11 February. Went to see Miss Feilding with Horatia. Found there Mr F. Went to do our shopping in a carriage, just the two of us. Lord and Lady Valletort came in the evening. Mr Mansel Talbot and John Strangways dined here. A little music in the evening. Extremely cold and gloomy weather.

Sunday 12 February. Went to mass at the Bavarian chapel with Horatia and Mr F., and Lord and Lady V. The music was not so good as last Sunday. Lord Kerry came. He said that the cholera is in London, at Rotherhithe on the Thames, with increase of troubles! Mr Feilding and Horatia went to dine with Caroline. Milady, Mr Talbot and I went to join them for the evening. Caroline showed us a very pretty pearl and emerald bracelet which her father-in-law Lord Mount Edgcumbe had given her, a necklace and ear-rings of gold and turquoise which were a present from her sister-in-law Lady Brownlow, a little box of antique gold from Lord Brownlow, a superb diamond circlet given by Sir Charles Lemon; it is a serpent which is biting its tail and in the middle is a very beautiful emerald. This jewel could serve as a scarf pin or as a Sévigné and is in the very best taste. The diamonds which she had from the late Countess of Mount Edgcumbe are quite good but they need remounting and cleaning. She will wear them at her presentation on the 24th. Lord Valletort gave her a very beautiful gold bracelet for her birthday, in the form of a Greek pattern. In fact she has had presents from all sides.

Monday 13. Gloomy weather, cold and rainy. 7 people were attacked by cholera in Rotherhithe. Yesterday I started to read *Notre Dame de Paris*, a curious novel by the novelist Victor Hugo. Went out in the carriage with Horatia to take some wedding cake from Caroline to Mrs Moore, their nurse, who was with Lady Burghish. We all went to Drury Lane Theatre, Milady, Mr F., Mr Talbot, Horatia, Lord and Lady Valletort, who came in passing just as we were sitting down at table and could not hear of the show without wishing to come too. She dressed with the help of her sister. Lord Kerry came and met us there. The show was rather insipid; it was *Rob Roy MacGregor*, very well acted, however, by Macready, who seems to be a very good actor – although I could not judge him in this role. He has a very clear pronunciation, he holds himself well, he has a relaxed manner, gracious and noble, and, although ugly and red-haired, has expressive features and piercing eyes, although blue. He gave me the impression of this personage so well described by Sir Walter Scott. Apart from him, the play is cold and bad. Mrs Wood (Miss Paton, the divorced wife of Lord William Lennox) played Diana Vernon, her much-praised voice is harsh and shrill. She gave us all the organ stops and deafening cries in that Scottish manner so like the *Highland Lad*. What taste!

However she was boisterously applauded by the galleries. After this we had again the *Little Thumb*, or *Hop o'my Thumb* again, a Harlequin farce, but not so well done as at Covent Garden. It was extremely cold in the theatre, which is so large that it is difficult to hear.

☞ *Tuesday 14*. The cholera continues at Rotherhithe, Limehouse and various little places on the river. 12 people have been attacked by it and 7 are dead.

☞ *Wednesday 15*. A ten-day quarantine has been imposed on the French coast for all vessels coming from this country. So long as this lasts I cannot dream of leaving. Lady Lansdowne, Lady Louisa Fitzmaurice and Mr Ch. Mansel Talbot dined here. They all went to Mrs Baring and to a ball given by the Princess Lieven. They talked of nothing but the cholera. Caroline was there, having dined with Lord Elliot. Her aunt, Lady Lansdowne, gave her a very beautiful pair of pearl ear-rings of fine pearls and Lord Lansdowne a necklace of gold links with chrysoprases with matching ear-rings, all of them very pretty.

☞ *Thursday 16*. I saw Dr Kerrisson, who found me a little better. The cholera has frightened away many people, who are leaving the city; others, who were coming, have changed their plans and are staying in the country. The merchants are beginning to cry aloud. There is talk of moving the parliament to Oxford or to Bath if the infection becomes dangerous; and Lady E. talks of leaving next week for Lacock. There is also some talk of postponing the Queen's drawing room, which should be held on the 24th. Lord and Lady Valletort came to dinner here. Caroline was gay, fresh and pretty. Mr John Strangways also came to dinner. Mr Feilding went in the evening to Lady Caroline Powlett's.

☞ *Friday 17 February*. Yesterday there were only four deaths from cholera; there is as yet nothing very frightening. The weather is always gloomy, cold, foggy and unhealthy. Went with Horatia to Boosey's, the music seller.

☞ *Saturday 18*. It was fine and we went out on foot, Horatia, Mr F. and myself to walk in Regents Park. The air was clear there and the sun, free from the clouds of smoke which obscure it in the streets, was shining brilliantly. We went as far as St Catherine's Hospital and met Lady Caroline Powlett on horseback. After lunch we went out in the carriage with Milady, shopping; went to Hardinge's and to Mortlock's, where there is some very beautiful porcelain and to Melmotte's, who is intolerably expensive. Lord Valletort came this evening before dinner. Caroline is not well. He had sent for Dr Kerrisson. Milady went to pass the evening with Mrs Cunliffe Offley.

☞ *Sunday 19 February*. The weather is gloomy and cold. It froze this evening. Went to see Caroline who is still in bed, although much better, then to Miss Feilding, who suffers much and has been bled. Milady returned to Caroline and found her worse; she could not dine with her guests. She was expecting to dinner today Lady Jemima and Lord Elliott, Lady Brownlow (sister of Lord Valletort). Mr Feilding and Horatia went also and then to a soirée at Lady Davy's and from there to Lady Sandwich. It was a fairly well employed Sunday – for an English Sunday. I am not feeling at all well this evening. The cholera has made scarcely any progress and the quarantine in France has been reduced from 10 to 5 days and finally to three. I have finished that extraordinary novel, *Notre Dame de Paris*; absurdly written, but not without some interest. Read a little of the *Chronicle* of Philip de Comines and of the *Chronicles* of Froissart. The terror created by the appearance of the cholera has begun to diminish. Many people arrived yesterday from the country, and the Queen's drawing room takes place on Friday the 24th as was originally arranged. Mr F. and Horatia dined at Caroline's with Lady Brownlow and Lady Jemima and Lord Elliot. Milady spent the evening with Lady Davy and Lady Sandwich, with Hor. and Mr F.

Monday 20. Long walk this morning with Mr F. and Horatia. Went to see Caroline for a moment who is still not very well. Mr John Strangways dined here. Milady went to see Caroline in the evening.

Tuesday 21. Mr F. went to Hampton Court. We visited Caroline this morning – she is better but looked weak and languid. Went to Boosey's for music. We were to go to the Olympic Theatre, but the good boxes were all taken; two remaining were too near the stage. Met this morning at Caroline's Sir Richard Vivian the great Anti-reformer and a Mr Glanville, friends of Lord Valletort. There are only two new cases of cholera at Southwark. The quarantine on the French coast is five days for vessels coming from the Thames. Started to read the memoirs of Giovanni Fiati. Mr John Strangways dined with us. Lady Glengall came this evening. Mr F. went to Lady Caroline Powlett.

Wednesday 22 February. Cold weather and gloomy. Thick yellow fog. I did not go out. Caroline came in for a moment this evening. She had been dining with Sir Charles Lemon. Mrs Nicholl came also to spend the evening. Milady and Mr Talbot went to Mrs Baring. Mr F. spent the evening out.

Thursday 23. The same cold fog. Caroline is going to be presented today to the Queen on the occasion of her marriage, but in private as a favour, because, tomorrow being the Queen's birthday, the Court congratulates her but it is not customary to be presented on that day. At first this favour of private presentation was regarded as very special, because up to now it has only been done for the wives of ambassadors – but it is much diminished by having been extended to Lady Ennismore (who had just married, as her second husband, the son of Lord Listowel), a person who is of no consideration. The Queen has also added the Marchioness of Ailsa, presented on the occasion of her new title, but at least one knows and respects her. The full court dress is not worn on these occasions, only a fine day dress. Yesterday the king held a levée. Mr Feilding went in his new uniform, in which he looks very well. The King was very well, and seemed gay. He complimented Mr F. on his daughter's marriage and joked with Lord Valletort on the subject. Lord V. looked very fine in the dress of the king's aide de camp. Caroline is still not well, which is a nuisance, because of the drawing room tomorrow.

Friday 24 February. [...] Yesterday went to Cartwright: consulted Dr Clarke (now Sir Charles Clarke) in the evening, who prescribed almost the same medicines as Dr Kerrisson. This morning I went to see Caroline dressed for the court (for the

Queen's birthday). She was very well dressed and looked very fine. She had the head-dress of white feathers which is obligatory here for the court; a very beautiful tiara on her forehead, made of one large pearl surrounded by diamonds; two long white [illegible] of diamonds, a large flower and an épin which looks very well in her dark hair; lappets of blonde lace. Her dress is of white satin, embroidered with silver in very rich rows and her train, according to the Queen's wish like a coronation robe; that is with a corsage open in front and joquettes and much more full than the ugly trains which have been worn until now, is of white velvet, lined with white silk and embroidered with silver. Plenty of blonde lace round the bodice and a breast-pin on the draperies of diamonds and emeralds. One single bracelet of emeralds and pearls; slippers of blonde below the [illegible]. She is extremely well thus and looks very noble. Lord Valletort is excessively good-looking in the dress uniform of the King's aide de camp. A red uniform, covered in gold.

Mrs Percy Fraser called in my absence and left her card. Milady has a dress of gold lamé, a silk train figured in green and a kind of toque in gold and green gauze with white feathers. Horatia was in a white dress, embroidered with green silk, which did not please me at all, and a train of white of gros de Naples, feathers and a huge Sévigné on her forehead, made of stones of all colours.

It was shocking weather – a thick yellow fog. They returned from the court very pleased with their reception. The King and Queen had been most gracious and had congratulated each member of the family individually on Caroline's marriage. The King said to Horatia that he had no doubt he would soon have to make her the same compliments on her own account. There were several superb outfits, they say; those of Lady Londonderry, of the Duchess of Bedford, of Lady Caroline Powlett, of Lady Jersey and Mrs Baring were dazzling, with gold and silver embroidery, diamonds, rubies, emeralds, sapphires etc. etc.

The fog became so thick this evening that it was like one of the plagues of Egypt. No carriages ventured into the street, and one could not see the lamps even at 20 paces. The few people who wandered into this sea of shadows cried out to warn each other of their coming. I have never seen anything like it and I was frightened and oppressed. I felt as if the shades would never disperse. Finally, it even filled the rooms of the house. Mr F. thought it would be a very bold thing to do to go to a ball at the Duke of Devonshire's – however, Milady was insistent and she and Horatia dressed for it and the carriage came at 11.30. The coachman thought he could go at a walking pace without danger and two men walked beside the carriage carrying long torches. It looked like a funeral procession. However, to our amazement, we found that this horrible fog was much less by midnight when they left. One could see the houses opposite and finally the mist became transparent, but before it had been like a coverlet of wool thrown over the whole town.

Saturday 25 February. They returned at 4.30 am. The ball was very nice, although not very crowded for Devonshire House. Caroline found herself too tired by her grand dinner with Lord Salisbury (with 24 Tories, she the only one of her party, poor child) to go to it. She goes today to Lord Mount Edgcumbe at Twickenham until Monday. We went out a little in the carriage; it was very cold. Lord Kerry dined here. He seemed not to be in bad health; he had a languid air which is not natural in one of his age. Apart from that he has improved in looks and has a very distinguished appearance. Played many duets in the evening.

Sunday 26 February. I meant to go and see Mrs Fraser this morning, but I was not much disposed to go out, above all to return by myself. It was cold and gloomy. Yesterday there were 15 new cases of cholera, of whom 13 have died. It is a rather frightening proportion! The quarantine in France for vessels from Dover is three days and ten for those coming from the Thames. Therefore I must abandon the idea of leaving while this lasts. Mrs William Mundy (Henrietta Frampton) is here. I went out with Milady in the carriage to make several visits, among others to Mrs Fraser, whom I did not find in; she was at Hampton Wick. Went to see Miss Matilda Feilding and Mrs Hicks. Horatia and Mr F. went to St James's where they heard the Bishop of London (Dr. Bloomfield) preach. Mr and Mrs Mundy and Sir Charles Lemon dine here today. Mr John Strangways came too. They went to spend the evening with Mrs Batthyani (formerly Mme de Bubna, wife of the Austrian governor of Milan). We had a little amateur music.

Monday 27 February. Walked with Mr F. and Horatia. We went to Tampon to see if she had returned from Richmond but we learned that Lord Valletort had been taken with an attack of gout and that they would not return until the evening. Went then to the Duchess of Gloucester (the King's sister) to hear news of her health; she has been very ill but she is better today. Went out later in the carriage with Milady – went to the Bazaar and again to Caroline who had just returned alone with her father-in-law, Lord Mount Edgcumbe. Poor Lord Valletort is very bad with his gout. She is dining with the king: her hair has been dressed and she should look very well; in a white satin gown, with her diamonds. Lord V. has stayed alone at Richmond: his father is also dining with the king. The others all went to Lady Powlett and to Lady Grey this evening who had a large soirée. Lord Grey had been tormented in the House of Lords and was said to have a gloomy air.

Tuesday 28 February. Caroline gives us very agreeable details of her dinner at St James's Palace yesterday. There were only 12 people there and they dined in the small apartments of the Queen, who was very friendly towards Caroline and wished to do her portrait in crayons. Lord Mount Edgcumbe was there, Lord and Lady Brownlow, Sir Andrew Barnard, Princess Augusta, Lord James O'Brien, Lord and Lady Wheatley etc. etc. Nothing could have been happier and more simple than the family life of this good king, who only slept for a short while after dinner, a wonderful thing for him!! Otherwise, poor Caroline is sad to be separated from her husband and to know that he is quite alone and suffering pain. Yesterday I saw Mrs Fraser passing in her carriage in Piccadilly and I greeted her. Wrote a long letter to Mrs Hopwood, answering all the reproaches and insinuations in her last one. I did not go out today. Mr and Mrs W. Mundy and Lord Kerry dined here. Caroline came this evening. Lord Valletort has returned and is better, but not well enough to go to the House of Commons, which annoys him considerably. Sir Charles Lemon came in during the day, determined to vote against the Government on the question of members for different parts of London; that is to say, 16 for the whole town, which has only four to represent 1,200,000 inhabitants! It is one of the clauses of the Reform Bill. It seems to me that it is not important enough for the Whigs to be voting against their own party. That is what they are like; they work constantly to undermine their own cause and are the first to check the Government and to oppose it. It is not thus that the Tories work who hold themselves together so well all the time.

Wednesday 29 February. The Ministry carried the day yesterday and had a majority of 80. It is said that several cases of cholera are not reported by the health authorities, so as not to alarm the people. However these poor doctors themselves fear the violence of the newspapers who persist in maintaining that they (the doctors) make a profit by spreading terror; since in the interests of commerce they do not like the quarantine and therefore they wish to persuade people that the cholera does not exist. I see in the papers that the steamships are beginning today to go from Southampton to Le Havre, as there is no quarantine from the west of Brighton. I am therefore very uncertain about my plans; it is a terrible crossing in this season. This evening Mrs Mundy went to Mrs Baring, very well dressed in a gown of black satin, with an ornament and a tiara of pink topazes, which suited her very well. Horatia went to spend the evening with her sister.

Thursday 1 March. Wrote to Mary, from whom I have received a very friendly letter from Knowsley this morning. Wrote a note to Mrs Fraser. Rain this morning. 26 cases of cholera yesterday and 12 people dead. They went to Lansdowne House where there was a great soirée, and to Mrs Bradshaw, where there was music. (Mrs Bradshaw was Miss Tree (actress): Maria Tree the pretty and agreeable young actress). Received a reply from Mrs Fraser.

Friday 2 March. Went to visit Mrs Fraser, who received me very kindly, although from time to time she expressed her annoyance, which didn't worry me at all. Caroline and Horatia dined with their aunt, Miss Feilding. Sent to Mary a French diary franked by Lord Auckland.

Saturday 3 March. Soirée at the Duchess of Dino's, to which Milady and Horatia went. Caroline dined here. Lord Valletort came this evening and he sang.

Sunday 4. This evening we had some music, with M. Tellier, secretary of the French ambassador, M. Tolstoy, a Russian gentleman attached to the embassy of the Prince of Lieven, il maestro Vaccoj, who sang several of his pretty canzonettas with plenty of taste but little voice. M. Tellier is an accomplished musician, sight-reads and accompanies very well. He sang the 'Barcarolle' from *Fra Diavolo* by Auber and one from *Robert the Devil* by Meyerbeer. M. Tolstoy sang some Russian airs. I sang, not very well, the duet 'Ah se de mali miei' by Rossini, with Vaccoj. The gentlemen sang the pirates' chorus from Horatia's opera *La sposa d'Abido* and that of Epithalamium from the same opera. Mr and Mrs Mundy, Sir Charles Lemon, Lord and Lady Valletort and Mr John Strangways came to spend the evening. They also sang Caroline's *Agnus Dei*. M. and Mme Puzzi sent no word and did not come.

Monday 5 March. Beautiful weather. Walked with Mr F. and Horatia. Met Lord and Lady Valletort at a saddler's shop. Went to the Olympic Theatre (Mme Vestris's theatre). They were playing *Woman's Revenge*, a fairly insignificant little play, in which Mrs Glover acted very well. Then we had the *Eleventh Day* (that is, the eleventh day of the marriage of an old bachelor). Liston is excellent in this part of a newly married man, which he fills with perfect naturalness and comedy. Mme Vestris plays the part of the young wife and plays it very well. She sings an Italian scene with a voice that makes one regret that she had not taken a bigger part. She also sang a French romance, fills alternately the role of a giddy young woman, then of a young man with pretensions and finally of a sort of French grisette – all this with plenty of vivacity and comedy. She is much altered. Nothing remains of her beauty but her smile, her eyes, which are superb and a perfect figure and proportions. Her arms and legs are admirable. This play is quite improbable but very amusing. Then we had *He is not a Miss*, a very gay piece of nonsense in which Liston is excellent. Then the *Olympic Devils* in which Mme Vestris played Orphée and showed in all their beauty her perfect legs. It is a classic farce. On leaving the box, I met Lady Vincent, who greeted me in a most agreeable manner.

Tuesday 6 March. I did not go out all day, but in the evening we went to the opera to see Donizetti's *L'Esule di Roma*, which was even weaker than his other productions. There is no interest in the poem, no charm or novelty in the music which is heavy, or, to put it better, recalls only a collection of well known pretty tunes which he has spoiled. The singers are no more than mediocre, except Mariani, who has a very good bass voice and a good method, though one could not have discerned that here. Also we had an idiotic diversion between the two acts of the opera and finally the ballet of the *Somnambulist* in which Albert danced; he does not seem to me to have changed at all and is still a most graceful dancer. The only service which Mr Monk Mason has rendered the opera is to increase the chorus and orchestra, which is infinitely better. The theatre has also been newly painted and has new hangings, but I do not at all like these brilliant green and the red draperies. Mr Danneskiold came to see us in our box, also Mr Charles Murray, Mr John Trotter etc. Saw Miss Ch. Dundas.

Wednesday 7 March. Caroline came in for a moment this morning. Milady and Horatia went to dine in Lansdowne House and Mr Talbot I know not where. I dined with Mr F. Afterwards they all went to Lady Tankerville's, where there was music. Had a note from Mrs Fraser who has left again for Kingston.

Thursday 8 March. Received a long letter from Mrs Hopwood. She has repented of her suspicions and insinuations. She tells me she has found me a companion for my journey, a Mlle de Longchamps who has been spending the winter with Lady Vincent at Deepdene and now wishes to return to Paris. That lady has also written to me; I shall go and see her tomorrow. Long walk. Mr F. and Horatia went to dinner with Caroline, who is not very well.

Friday 9. Went to see the *Panorama of Florence* with Horatia, her father and her uncle John. I was disappointed with it. They have given that beautiful town a

The Swiss city of Berne was used by the Talbots and Amélina as their base during their six-month continental tour in 1833-34

shabby appearance. The whole thing looks small, crowded, confused and does not give at all a good impression of it. The banks of the Arno are well shown and the air is quite southern, the sun brilliant. Went to see the improvements in the Strand which is now a very fine street. St Martin's Church has been quite cleared of the ruins which formerly hid it and the new passage called the Lowther Arcade, which is very pretty. They are working there without respite. Wrote a note to Mlle de Longchamps to ask if the ladies were alone this evening. She replied that she was afraid not, and that she would come tomorrow morning. Mr John Strangways dined here. Milady, Horatia and Mr F. went to a musical soirée with music at Lord Burghersh's.

Saturday 10. Mlle de Longchamps came this morning to find out if I could arrange to leave with her for Paris. I have not decided anything. Saw Mrs Herbert and Lady Vincent. They were very friendly to me, I shall go to see them. Mrs Mundy and Sir Charles Lemon came this morning. Lord and Lady Valletort are dining here, also Lord Auckland.

Ten days later Amelina set out for France.

Tuesday 20 March 1832. I left London at 10 o'clock in the morning after having said sad farewells to my dear Horatia and Mr F. I took leave of Caroline and Milady the night before.

After six months with her family in France, Amélina returned briefly to Lacock and then London, where Caroline's first child was born in November, before going once more to live at Hopwood.

⓪ I left Brunoy on 15 September 1832, and Paris on the 18th: arrived in London on the 21st, where I found Mr Feilding, and left again for Laycock, where I was very happy for three weeks: then we left there again with Lady Valletort and Lady Elisabeth, for London.

⓪ On the 5th of November 1832, Monday, Caroline brought a son into the world, her first-born! and this event gave me one of the sweetest moments of my life.

William Henry Fox Talbot, Lady Elisabeth's son by her first marriage, was married to Constance Mundy in December 1832. Their wedding tour was delayed by his duties as MP for Chippenham, but in January 1833 he wrote to Amélina at Hopwood Hall, inviting her to accompany them to France, Switzerland and Italy. Her delight at this invitation is evident from her reply on 15 January 1833:

'I cannot well express the joy that your last letter made me feel! Your proposition which still seems to me the result of one of my dreams, enchants me so much that I feel quite a different person since I have received it. However I am afraid to place too much reliance on such a flattering hope; the disappointment would be cruel and I find myself inventing obstacles which make me doubt if this delightful plan can come to be. I cannot thank you enough for your kindness to me in joining me to your pleasant society, but in truth I have received so many favours from your dear family that a new mark of your care for me, though it adds to my gratitude can add nothing to such great affection as I feel for you. I include Mrs Talbot among the number of those who have so much right to my gratitude and I beg you ask her to accept my affectionate respect, in expressing to her the lively desire I feel to have the benefit of knowing her, and my thanks for the choice she has made of me as one of the party of three. I shall be entirely at your disposal at any time you care to arrange, for leaving and returning. I have nothing to keep me here, quite the contrary, this plan puts an end for the moment to painful concern for the future: but I shall see you to make our final arrangements. I shall be at Laycock Abbey at the latest towards the end of March and then we shall have time to make arrangements together.'

⓪ *13 March.* I left Hopwood on 13 March and arrived at Laycock on the 14th, very content to find myself there once more. Caroline and Lord Valletort were there with their dear little child, whom I found improved in looks: he is not very fat, but he is chubby, blooming, in good health, and in such good humour that he hardly ever cries; he is a charming child, and all the family dote upon him. Lord and Lady Valletort had come from Windsor where the King had invited them to spend several days. Among other people there were Namiek Pacha, the Turkish envoy, an educated man, speaking European languages well, and superior to those of his compatriots who have been sent up to now to foreign courts.

We left Laycock on 15 April 1833 for London.

After spending a few weeks in London, Talbot and his wife Constance, accompanied by Amélina as travelling companion and by their servants, set out for the continent in June 1833.

∞ *20 June 1833:* I left London with Mr. and Mrs. Talbot; this trip had been planned for six months. I parted with regret from Horatia and her excellent parents, we had delightful weather as far as Dover, where we slept at the Ship Hotel, which they had rebuilt after it had been burned down, and which consequently is not yet very comfortable. We dined earlier in Rochester. From Blackheath as far as Canterbury we seemed to be travelling on flowers, the air was so scented with their perfume and I asked why we should go so far with such effort to look for a beautiful country. [...]

From Boulogne they went on to Paris and from there to Dijon. Crossing the Jura to Switzerland they visited Neufchatel before settling in Berne, from where they made several excursions, for example to the recently completed St. Gotthard pass (built 1820–1830). In the canton of Ticino they visited the Val Levantina, Bellinzona and finally, for a short rest, Magadino on Lago Maggiore. Then the arduous journey continued through the Swiss mountains to the summit of St. Bernardino. An enthusiastic botanist and fellow of the Linnean Society, Talbot was greatly interested in the alpine flora.

∞ 2 August 1833: Mr. T. made us get up early although we did not leave until a quarter past ten, having spent two hours drying his flowers [...] we continued to ascend for two hours on a good twisting road in countryside wilder than everything I had seen, always with the exception of the St. Gotthard with its terrible Schoellenen and the Val Tremola, which I shall never forget. I again walked a great deal, a considerable amount even for me, always taking short cuts: all this with a biting wind of extreme violence, and a little fine rain, having arrived at the top of the St. Bernardino, at the height of the perpetual snows, it was difficult to walk, the wind which blew from the glaciers of the Muttnerhorn was so freezing. The summits of the other mountains were wrapped in clouds and mists. We found quantities of beautiful alpine flowers [...] Mrs T. and I had practically lost the use of our legs. [...] Mrs. T. is tiring herself too much. She is walking a lot, sleeps badly, and hardly eats anything. She was greatly changed yesterday and ended by falling ill. As for myself I am hardly any better. I no longer dare to eat anything. [...] This village of Spluegen is 3000 feet above sea level. They work the white marble there which is found abundantly in the mountains. The rain continues and the sky is dark: I am fearful for tomorrow.

∞ 3 August 1833: When I opened my eyes at five o'clock a brilliant sun was lighting up a peak covered with snow which I could see from my bed. I got up immediately to enjoy this beautiful view and to survey the length of this valley of Rheinwald.

When they crossed to Italy, magic awaited them on Lake Como:

∞ Wednesday, 25 September 1833: We went in our boat, taken on the blue waters by our little boys to the Villa Melzi, [...] we saw there all the flowers and rare trees in detail: I saw beautiful pomegranate trees bearing fruit which was quite ripe. The gardener gave us a very big one. There was an Olea fragrens which has a delicious smell [...] the magnolias there of a height and breadth much more considerable than any I have ever seen: myrtle, laurel and oleander grew there in profusion. […] While Mr. T. was examining all these curiosities with delight, I asked the intelligent gardener who showed them to us to take me once more to see the fine portrait of Napoleon by Appiani. […] We went to the Lavedo promontory where Mrs. T. did two views of the Villa Balbiana, we during this time letting ourselves rock gently on the waves. Then we returned to Cadenabbia and having climbed up behind the house among the vines we made several drawings there. I did one of the beautiful majestic Villa Melzi. The weather was glorious and tonight after dinner we went by moonlight to sit on the steps of the Villa Sommariva and to walk to Tremezzo. This country, the weather, the sun, the artifacts and the charming buildings […] it is a scene of perpetual enchantment. What a shame then to leave it. [...] We were literally on our feet the whole day so were are very tired and we are going to bed at 10 o.clock

Throughout the six months of the journey the ladies in the party filled their sketch books with drawings of their surroundings. While in Nice, for example, Amélina notes:

- *14 November 1833:* Went to draw with Mrs. T. on the road to Cimier.
- *16 November 1833*: Went with Caroline and Mme T. to Cimier on donkeys. They both did a view of the picturesque monastery of Recollets.
- *21 November 1833:* Went walking with Mme. T. as far as S. Ponzo, of which we made a little drawing.

After the rigours of their travels, which often involved fighting bitterly cold weather and staying in dirty inns, the travellers finally arrived back in Paris in December 1833, where they lodged at the Hotel de la Terrace. Amélina was able to see her mother and stepfather, and there were many visits to the opera and the shops.

- *19 December 1833*: Mrs. T. has bought a very beautiful dress of yellow silk richly brocaded at Delisle's and a hat at Mme. Thomas's. The shops are extremely brilliant, there is a big crowd in the streets and Paris looks animated and gay; but for ourselves we have no other pleasure there than the sight of these wonderful things.

The subsequent journey back to London and eventually to Lacock was not easy in the piercing cold of winter.

- *Monday, 6 January 1834.* We got up again at 4 o'clock in the morning to embark at 6. We left the port of Calais at half past six, there was very little wind from the S.W. but a heavy sea: we lay down on our beds immediately and were very ill: the movement was violent, happily we did not have a storm but 4 and a half hours of suffering! It was the darkest night you could imagine and I could not help shuddering on boarding this little ship, which seemed like a tomb: half an hour later we would not have had enough water to get into the harbour. We rested at the Ship Inn at Dover, while our baggage was examined by customs, then we set off again all very unwell for Sittingbourne where we slept at the George Hotel.
- *Saturday 11.* Left London at 9 o'clock all three in the coupé: Dined in the good inn at Speenhill. It was fine until 2 o'clock then much rain and a violent wind on

1834

Marlborough Hill and Cherhill. Arrived at Laycock Abbey at 11 o'clock at night. There were Lady Harriet Galway, her three daughters and Mr and Mrs Traherne: Horatia is fine and bonny. Milady and Mr F have bad colds: I was very happy to see them again: many of the visitors had gone.

For the time being I will leave this diary: unless something special occurs to be recorded.

My health continues good and I have this obligation to Mr and Mrs Talbot whose company I am sorry to lose, for here I will not see her so intimately. The family here speak of going to the continent to rejoin Caroline next April and to let the house in London. They should be away a year.

The Galways and Trahernes have gone. Lord Henry FitzMaurice came to dine here. Today we have Mr Tom Liddell; Horatia and Mr Fielding have gone to Compton Basset to Mrs Heneage. The weather is still dreadful.

Thursday 16 January. The steam-boat the *Belfast* has run aground on the sandbanks at Calais, happily no-one perished.

Mr Tom Liddell, the second son of Lord Ravensworth, left us last Monday, he is very likeable and draws wonderfully, likes flowers, music and has been the only architect of the houses of his father and two of his brothers-in-law. He is going to his sister Lady Barrington who sings so well and is so pretty.

Thursday 23 January 1834. I read during the last week the 11th volume of the memoirs of the Dsse. d'Abrantés. It is difficult to meet in a single work with so much collected nonsense! She judges everything through foolish spectacles, men, society, the most important facts: and if occasionally she amuses, there followed immediately the thought that it is only at the expense of truth.

I have read *Indiana*, a really fashionable novel by George Sand: the style is romantic, that is all that need be said, and the facts quite interesting but unbelievable and based on the most revolting principles: suicide is advocated coldly by a virtuous man who nevertheless does not kill himself and even ends by being very happy with a woman who has rejected every obligation. [...] this is Indiana, who has caused the suicide of her maid, the death of her husband after having wished to kill herself, and spent several years ruled by a violent passion for a real scoundrel! [...] Such are the latest books! – to take a rest from this dismal reading, I took *Raoul ou l'Enéide*, a charming little novel by Mme Bawr, with a simple flowing style, natural incidents, pure morals, in short it is an excellent work especially after *Indiana*! I have just started *Rome souterraine*, a novel by M. Charles Didier; I think I shall like it perhaps only because of the setting where he has placed his characters in Rome and in the Campagna!

February 17. Sunday. Mr Feilding has been horribly unwell for three weeks: First he had rheumatism in his cheek, now it is gout in one knee and alternatively in both feet. He has not left his room for about a week and can hardly leave his bed. He suffers patiently; but it is easy to see that his constitution is changing which makes me very sad; he changes every day: however I found him looking better today. They had promised to take me if they went away.[...]

The Hopwoods, who are excellent people, have kept up their interest in me and have not forgotten me. Mrs Hopwood writes to engage me to go and see them as soon as possible in the most friendly terms.

Caroline is still at Nice; she will be confined next August: she will stay on the continent for this event; and that is what will decide her family to go and join her.

☙ *Sunday 23 March 1834*. Had news from Mrs Hopwood a few days ago. She tells me that Frank is still received with open arms at Knowsley and that his marriage with Miss Stanley is arranged but will not take place until he has taken orders and has a living. They are all overjoyed. I am awaiting with impatience news of Mary and hope to hear of a happy outcome. [...]

I am thinking of going to Brunoy. The family here leave to go and spend the summer in Geneva on the 27 of May or the 5th of June next; then they will go for the winter to Nice. Caroline has settled on Geneva for her lying-in. So I shall go about the same time, a little earlier if I can: for Brunoy or for Hopwood Hall.

☙ *Thursday 27 March 1834*. I was very happy this morning to receive a letter from dear little Mary Hopwood who tells me in terms of the liveliest and most natural joy that her marriage is arranged with Lord Molyneux (son of Lord Sefton); but she has not yet told me the date: I have written to her immediately to congratulate her. She has loved him for a long time, she has known him almost from the cradle. I have arranged to accept the kind invitation of Mrs Hopwood and of Mary immediately.

☙ *Thursday 24 April*. Mr and Mrs Talbot have gone to settle in London last Monday in Mr Feilding's house in Sackville St. They will stay there during the parliamentary session; that is to say until the middle of July. Mr Feilding has left this morning for London where he is going to say goodbye to his sisters and to his friends and to put his affairs in order before his departure.

☙ *Thursday 8 May 1834* I left Laycock Abbey for Bath on the way to Hopwood Hall.

This was the last visit to Lacock recorded in Amélina's journals, and it seems that she feared she might never live there again. In fact she was to be intimately involved with Henry Talbot's family for most of the rest of her life, as his business agent in Paris when he began to market his photographic method, and then at Lacock as companion to his wife and children, until she died there, an honoured member of the household, in 1876.

Principal People and Places

LORD AUCKLAND, EDEN GEORGE (1784–1849). Family friend. Whig politician, Master of the Mint, First Lord of the Admiralty in 1834. Governor General of India 1835–41. Vice-president of Horticultural and Zoological Society. Trustee of British Museum.

JOHN AWDRY. Steward at Lacock. Lived at Lackham House, Notton, with his family, 2 miles NW of Lacock.

WILLIAM LISLE BOWLES (1762–1850). Vicar of Bremhill from 1804. He was well known as a poet and formed part of the literary circle at Bowood and Lacock.

HENRY JOHN GEORGE HERBERT, 3rd Earl of Carnarvon (1800–49). Family friend. Travel writer and excellent linguist. Elected Tory MP for Wootton Bassett, Wiltshire in 1831. Family seat – Highclere in Hampshire.

SIR CHRISTOPHER COLE (1770–1836). Captain in the Royal Navy. Married Lady Mary Lucy Talbot (1776–1855), widow of Thomas Mansel Talbot of Penrice Castle and sister of Lady Elisabeth Feilding. Lady Mary was a very keen gardener and inspired a love of botany in her nephew, William Henry Fox Talbot.

JOHN NICHOLAS FAZAKERLEY (1787–1852). Whig MP. Friend and travel companion of the Feildings.

CHARLES FEILDING (1780–1835). Naval Captain, later Rear Admiral. Married the widowed Lady Elisabeth Theresa Talbot in 1804. William Henry Fox Talbot's stepfather and father of Caroline and Horatia. Descended from the Hapsburg family (Geoffrey of Rheinfelden). Friend of King William IV, who was a naval officer himself. Frequently referred to in Amélina's journals as *Mr F.*

CAROLINE AUGUSTA FEILDING (1808–81). Daughter of Lady Elisabeth Feilding and half-sister to William Henry Fox Talbot. Married Ernest August Valletort, 3rd Earl of Mount Edgcumbe, in February 1832 at Bowood House. She became mother to three children and resided at Mount Edgcumbe and later Cotehele. Talented sketcher and musician. Often referred to in Amélina's journals as *Tampon.*

LADY ELISABETH THERESA FEILDING, née FOX STRANGWAYS (1773–1846). Eldest daughter of the 2nd Earl of Ilchester. Married William Davenport Talbot in 1796. Their son William Henry Fox Talbot was born in 1800. After her husband's death later that year, she married Charles Feilding in 1804 and they had two daughters, Caroline and Horatia. Interested in the arts, science, music and travel. Frequently referred to in Amélina's journals as *Lady E.* or *Milady.*

HENRIETTA HORATIA MARIA FEILDING (1810–51). Half-sister of William Henry Fox Talbot. Gifted musician. Married Capt. Thomas Gaisford. Died in childbirth, but her only child survived.

MR AND MRS FORD: Friends of Lady Elisabeth Feilding. Lived at Pickwick Lodge.

LADY HARRIOT FRAMPTON (1778–1844). Sister of Lady Feilding. Married to James Frampton of Moreton. Known as the 'intellectual sister' in the family.

GIOVANNINA. Italian servant at Lacock Abbey.

REV. JOHN GUTHRIE. Vicar of Calne. Tutor of Lord Kerry of Bowood House.

LT. COL. JOHN TORRIANO HOULTON (1773–1839). Lived with his family at Farley Castle, outside Bath. Interested in geology. His daughters shared their musical interests with the Feilding girls.

MR AND MRS ROBERT HOPWOOD and **MARY HOPWOOD** of Hopwood Hall, near Manchester. Amélina spent several years with the family as a companion to Mary. Mr Hopwood was a friend of Byron who stayed at Hopwood Hall in 1811. Byron's nephew 'Captain Leigh' stayed at Hopwood while Amélina was there.

LADY ILCHESTER (1771–1842). Lived at Melbury, Dorset. Lady Elisabeth Feilding's step-mother.

LORD KERRY, WILLIAM THOMAS FITZMAURICE (1811–36). Lord Lansdowne's elder son and heir. Went to Westminster school, took his MA at Cambridge, became an MP in 1832. Died at the age of 25.

LADY LANSDOWNE, LOUISA EMMA (1785–1851). Wife of Lord Lansdowne. Younger sister of Lady Elisabeth Feilding. Patron of literature and art, interested in music, medieval history and education. Hostess to many important literary and political figures of the age such as Mme de Staël, Maria Edgeworth, and Lord John Russell. Mother of three children, Lord Kerry, Lady Louisa, and Lord Henry, William Henry Fox Talbot's cousins.

LORD LANSDOWNE, HENRY PETTY-FITZMAURICE, 3RD MARQUESS (1780–1863). Lady Elisabeth Feilding's brother-in-law. Whig politician, champion of Catholic Emancipation and of the abolition of the slave-trade. Interests in music, literature, art, architecture, travel and the sciences. Appointed Lord President of the Council in 1835. First president of the Bath (Royal) Literary and Scientific Institution (1825). Resided at Bowood House and at Lansdowne House in London.

Lady Lemon, Charlotte Ann (1784–1826). Sister of Lady Elisabeth Feilding and wife of **Sir Charles Lemon**, MP, President of the Royal Cornwall Polytechnic Society, and owner of Carclew House.

Mr and Mrs Paul Methuen. Neighbours and friends of the Feilding family, resided at Corsham Court.

George Stephen Montgomerie (1790–1850). Norfolk clergyman, friend and travelling companion of the Feildings. Rector of Garboldisham 1815–50.

Thomas Moore (1779–1852). Born in Dublin, son of a grocer, educated at Trinity College. Published the successful *Irish Melodies*, which established him as the national poet of Ireland. Good musician and skilful writer of patriotic and nostalgic songs (e.g. *The Minstrel Boy* and *The Last Rose of Summer*). Became famous throughout Europe with the publication of *Lalla Rookh* in 1817. Lived in a cottage in Sloperton near Melksham with his wife and children. A lively and respected member of the literary and musical circle at Bowood and Lacock. Friend of Byron, whose biography he published in 1830.

Morphine. Mr Feilding's dog, found in Genoa at the Piazza Fontana Amorosa during the family's travels in Italy in 1823.

Sir William Francis Patrick Napier (1785–1860). Colonel Napier was a military historian, served in Spain in the Peninsula War. Author of *The History of the War in the Peninsula*. Received a knighthood in 1848 and was promoted to General in 1859. Lived with his family in Bromham, Wiltshire.

Rev. James Paley (1790–1863). Son of Archdeacon Paley of Carlisle. Vicar at Lacock

William Fox Strangways (1795–1865). Lady Elisabeth Feilding's half-brother, eldest son of the second Earl of Ilchester by his second wife. Diplomat with postings in Vienna, Italy and Frankfurt. Botanist. Keen collector of Italian Renaissance paintings who donated his collection to the Ashmolean Museum in Oxford. In 1858 he became the 4th Earl of Ilchester.

Constance Talbot, née Mundy (1811–80). From Markeaton Hall, Derbyshire, married

William Henry Fox Talbot in 1832. Amélina accompanied the newly married couple on their delayed wedding tour of the continent in 1833. The Talbots had three daughters and one son.

William Henry Fox Talbot (1800–77). Lady Elisabeth Feilding's only son, from her marriage to William Davenport Talbot. Known as Henry in the family and a much loved half-brother of Caroline and Horatia Feildlng. Educated at Harrow and Cambridge. Travelled extensively as a young man, meeting many scientific men in Italy, France, Austria, Switzerland and Germany. Married Constance Mundy in 1832. Inherited the Lacock Abbey estate when he reached 21 but only settled in the Abbey in 1827 with his family. Accomplished in many scientific fields and an excellent mathematician. Fellow of the Royal Society at the age of 32. His interest in optics led him to the discovery of the negative/positive process, which allowed multiple photographic images to be created from a single negative, making him the father of English photography. Often referred to in Amélina's journals as *Mr T*.

Tampon. A pet name for Caroline Feilding.

Lord Valletort, Ernest August (1797–1861). Viscount, later Lord Mount Edgcumbe on his father's death in 1839. Received the Waterloo medal in 1816. Tory MP. Married Caroline Feilding in 1831. Settled an annuity on Amélina as a present for his bride Caroline on their wedding day. Enjoyed travelling but often afflicted by gout. Aide-de-camp to William IV.

Places mentioned by Amélina

Abbotsbury, Dorset. A village on the south coast of England between Weymouth and Bridport. Here the Ilchesters had a summer residence, known as Abbotsbury Castle.

Bowood House. Family residence of Lord and Lady Lansdowne, near Calne in Wiltshire.

Brunoy. Residence of Amélina's mother near Paris after her second marriage.

Corsham Court. Residence of the Methuen family in Corsham, Wiltshire.

Hopwood House. Home of the Hopwood family in Middleton, Manchester.

31 Sackville Street. London residence of the Feildings.

Melbury House. Residence of the Fox-Strangways family twelve miles from Dorchester in Dorset. William Henry Fox Talbot was born here.